Preface

The fields of Cloud Computing and the Internet of Things (IoT) represent some of the most dynamic and rapidly evolving areas in today's technological landscape. As integral components of modern computing, they are reshaping industries, driving innovation, and creating new opportunities for businesses and individuals alike. Recognizing their importance, the Indira Gandhi National Open University (IGNOU) has incorporated these subjects into its curriculum, challenging students to master both theoretical knowledge and practical skills.

This book, IGNOU Cloud Computing and IoT Previous Years Unsolved Papers, is a carefully curated compilation of unsolved question papers from previous years. It is designed to serve as an essential resource for students who are preparing for their exams in these subjects. The primary objective of this book is to provide students with a comprehensive tool to self-assess their understanding, identify areas for improvement, and refine their problem-solving skills.

We believe that practicing with previous years' question papers is one of the most effective ways to prepare for exams. It not only familiarizes students with the types and formats of questions they are likely to encounter but also helps them develop a deeper understanding of the subject matter by applying concepts to real-world scenarios. By working through these unsolved papers, students will be able to gauge their readiness, improve their time management during exams, and build confidence in tackling challenging questions.

The decision to leave the papers unsolved was intentional. We want students to engage actively with the material, think critically, and explore multiple approaches to solving the problems presented. This method encourages independent learning and ensures that students are better prepared to adapt to various question formats and difficulties during the actual exams.

This book covers a wide range of topics within Cloud Computing and IoT, including cloud architecture, service models, IoT protocols, security issues, and real-world applications. Each paper has been meticulously selected to ensure a comprehensive coverage of the syllabus, providing students with a thorough understanding of the core concepts required for success in their exams.

We hope that this book will not only assist students in their academic journey but also inspire them to delve deeper into these exciting fields. As technology continues to advance, the knowledge and skills gained in Cloud Computing and IoT will undoubtedly play a crucial role in shaping the future.

We would like to extend our gratitude to the faculty members and students of IGNOU who have contributed to the development of this book. Your feedback and insights have been invaluable in ensuring that this book meets the needs of today's learners.

Wishing you success in your studies and your future endeavors in the world of Cloud Computing and IoT.

Table of Contents

MCS – 227

Master Of Computer Applications (MCA)

Chapter 1: Term-End Examination, June,2022

MCS-227: Cloud Computing and IoT

Time: 3 Hours
Maximum Marks: 100
Weightage: 70

Note: (i) Question No. 1 is compulsory.
(ii) Answer any three Questions from the rest.

1. (a) Define Cloud Computing. List and explain the four categories of cloud deployment models. 10

(b) Define resource sharing in cloud computing. Explain the implementation of single-tenancy and multi-tenancy types of resource sharing in cloud computing. 10

(c) What is Internet of Things (IOT) ? What are the characteristics ? Also explain industrial IoT, infrastructure IoT and internet of military things (IoMT) categories of IoT. 10

(d) Explain the differences between Fog computing and Edge computing. Draw the block diagram of 3-layer architecture of fog computing and explain all its layers. 10

2. (a) Differentiate between cluster, grid and cloud computing with respect to its characteristics, physical structure, hardware, resources, applications, networking and scalability features. 10

(b) What is Auto scaling in cloud ? Write and explain fixed amount auto scaling algorithm. 10

3. (a) Define resource pooling in cloud environment. In this context, explain the following : 10
(i) Server Pools
(ii) Storage Pools
(iii) Network Pools

(b) With the help of a block diagram, explain the 4-levels in a cloud architecture. 10

4. (a) Define virtualization. Explain its underlying abstraction. Also mention the features provided by virtualization environment. 10

(b) Explain the following communication protocols with reference to the IoT devices: 10
(i) IPv6
(ii) MQTT
(iii) CoAP
(iv) XMPP

5. Write short notes on the following: 5*4 = 20
(a) Multihoming and its types
(b) Horizontal scaling in cloud environment
(c) Challenges in cloud computing
(d) Applications of edge computing

MCS – 227

Master Of Computer Applications (MCA)

Chapter 2: Term-End Examination, Dec,2022

MCS-227: Cloud Computing and IoT

Time: 3 Hours
Maximum Marks: 100
Weightage: 70

Note: (i) Question No. 1 is compulsory.
(ii) Answer any three Questions from the rest.

1. (a) What is resource provisioning in cloud computing ? Explain the static and dynamic approaches of resource provisioning. Mention their advantages and disadvantages. 10

(b) Define Load Balancing. Explain the following algorithms with reference to load balancing : 10
(i) Static algorithm approach
(ii) Weighted Round Robin

(c) Discuss the following baseline technologies of 1oT : 10
(i) Security in IoT
(ii) IoT Analytics
(iii) IoT Processors
(iv) IoT

(d) Define Edge Computing. Draw a block diagram of Cloud-Fog-Edge collaboration and explain all its layers. 10

2.(a) What is scalability in Cloud Computing ? 10
Explain the following strategies of scaling :
(i) Proactive Scaling
(ii) Reactive Scaling

(b) Define VM (Virtual Machine) sizing. Discuss the two ways to do VM sizing. 5

(c) Mention any five applications of Cloud Computing. 5

3. (a) Define a sensor with reference to an IoT device. Explain various characteristics of sensors. Also, mention and explain any four classifications of sensors. 10

(b) Explain the following computing components used in laboratories of IoT/Cloud : 10
(i) Arduino
(ii) Raspberry Pi

4. (a) Discuss the following Service Delivery Models of Cloud, with an example for each : 10
(i) Platform as a Service (PaaS)
(ii) Infrastructure as a Service (IaaS)

(b) "Cloud Computing offers a variety of deployment models, a network connection viewpoint will be used to examine Cloud deployment models and their accessible components." With reference to this statement, discuss the following types of network connectivities : 10
(i) Public Inter Cloud Networking
(ii) Private Intra Cloud Networking

5. Write short notes on the following : 4*5=20

(a) Applications of Fog Computing

(b) Desktop Level Virtualization

(c) Actuator and its any three types

(d) Zigbee, NFC and RFID connectivity technologies used in IoT applications.

MCS – 227

Master Of Computer Applications (MCA)

Chapter 3: Term-End Examination, June,2023

MCS-227: Cloud Computing and IoT

Time: 3 Hours
Maximum Marks: 100
Weightage: 70

Note: (i) Question No. 1 is compulsory.
(ii) Answer any three Questions from the rest.

1. (a) What is cloud computing service delivery models ? List and explain any four service delivery models. 10

(b) Explain the following scaling strategies : 10
(i) Proactive scaling
(ii) Reactive scaling
(iii) Combinational scaling
Also, compare proactive and reactive scaling with reference to the suitability, working, cost and implementation parameters.

(c) Explain all the four components, which support IoT system, with the help of a sample block diagram. 10

(d) What is fog computing ? Explain the working of its along with any use case. Also, mention it advantages. 10

2. (a) Define edge computing. Also, briefly explain the working of edge computing. 10
(b) What is Virtualization ? Explain its underlying abstraction. Also, mention important characteristics. 10

3. (a) Compare and contrast cluster, grid and cloud computing with reference to physical characteristics, structure, hardware, resources, applications, networking and scalability parameters. 10

(b) What is load balancing? What is its functionality? Explain the following load-balancers along with their features: 10
(i) Network load balancer
(ii) Application load balancer

4. (a) Define a sensor with reference to an IoT device. Explain its characteristics. List and explain any four IoT sensors along with their functions in the IoT devices. 10

(b) What is cloud security ? What are the threats to cloud security ? Explain various information security methods is cloud computing. 10

5. Write short notes on the following : 4*5=20
(a) Public and private clouds
(b) Challenges in cloud computing
(c) Hierarchical structure of cloud
(d) Use case of edge computing

MCS – 227

Master Of Computer Applications (MCA)

Chapter 4: Term-End Examination, Dec,2023

MCS-227: Cloud Computing and IoT

Time: 3 Hours
Maximum Marks: 100
Weightage: 70

Note: (i) Question No. 1 is compulsory.
(ii) Answer any three Questions from the rest.

1. (a) With reference to the Cloud Architecture, explain the following layers : 10
   (i) Client access layer
   (ii) Internet connectivity leyer
   (iii) Cloud service management layer
   (iv) Layer of physical resources

(b) What is load-balancing ? Why is it imperative in cloud computing to balance the cloud-load ? Also, explain briefly hardware-based load balancer and virtual load balancer. 10
(c) List and explain any ten emerging IoT technologies. 10
(d) What is Edge Computing ? Explain its working with the help of a use-case. 10

2. (a) Explain the following IoT-connectivity technologies : 10
(i) Zigbee
(ii) Z-wave
(iii) RFID
(iv) NFC
(b) With reference to cloud-security, explain the following : 10
(i) Identity management
(ii) Access control mechanism

3. (a) Explain any five applications of cloud computing. 5
(b) Write a short note on utility computing. 5
(c) Explain the evolution of cloud computing. 5
(d) Describe briefly the Hybrid-Cloud Deployment Model. 5

4. (a) What is machine or server level virtualization ? Briefly explain the following types of server level virtualization: 10
(i) Hypervisor
(ii) Full-virtualization

(b) Explain the following sensors used in 10T devices along with its features and applications : 10
(i) Image sensors
(ii) Chemical sensors
(iii) Acceleration sensors
(iv) Proximity sensors

5. Write short notes on the following . 4x5=20
(a) Actuators and its types
(b) MQTT, CoAP and XMPP 10T protocols
(c) Challenges of IoT
(d) Applications of fog computing

Chapter 5: Most Asked Questions Part-A

1. What is Cloud Computing, and how does it work?
Answer: Cloud Computing is the delivery of computing services—including servers, storage, databases, networking, software, and analytics—over the internet ("the cloud"). Instead of owning physical infrastructure, users access resources on-demand via service providers such as Amazon Web Services (AWS), Microsoft Azure, or Google Cloud. It operates on a pay-as-you-go model, which means users only pay for what they use. Cloud computing is categorized into three service models: Infrastructure as a Service (IaaS), Platform as a Service (PaaS), and Software as a Service (SaaS). It provides scalability, cost-effectiveness, flexibility, and increased collaboration, making it ideal for modern businesses and applications.

2. What are the different types of Cloud Deployment Models?
Answer: Cloud deployment models define how cloud services are made available to users. There are four main types: (1) Public Cloud – operated by third-party providers, offering resources to multiple customers over the internet; (2) Private Cloud – used exclusively by one organization, hosted internally or by a third party; (3) Hybrid Cloud – a combination of public and private clouds that share data and applications; (4) Community Cloud – shared by several organizations with common interests. Each model offers different levels of security, management, and scalability, depending on business requirements and compliance needs.

3. What is the role of virtualization in Cloud Computing?
Answer: Virtualization is a foundational technology in cloud computing that allows multiple virtual machines (VMs) to run on a single physical server. It enables the abstraction of hardware resources such as CPU, memory, and storage, making it easier to allocate, scale, and manage computing power efficiently. Virtualization provides benefits like increased resource utilization, cost reduction, flexibility, and simplified disaster recovery. Tools like VMware, KVM, and Microsoft Hyper-V are commonly used. It also facilitates the rapid provisioning of environments, which is essential for DevOps and cloud-native applications.

4. What are the advantages of Cloud Computing?
Answer: Cloud computing offers several advantages: (1) Cost efficiency – reduces capital expenses by eliminating the need for on-premise infrastructure; (2) Scalability – resources can be scaled up or down easily; (3) Accessibility – data and applications are accessible from anywhere with internet access; (4) Disaster recovery – built-in redundancy and backup capabilities; (5) Automatic updates – service providers maintain and update software and hardware; (6) Collaboration – teams can collaborate in real-time; and (7) Security – many providers offer robust security measures including encryption, compliance, and monitoring tools. These benefits make cloud computing an ideal choice for modern IT solutions.

5. What is Internet of Things (IoT)?
Answer: The Internet of Things (IoT) refers to the interconnection of physical devices—such as sensors, actuators, appliances, vehicles, and more—via the internet, enabling them to collect and exchange data. IoT systems consist of four main components: devices/sensors, connectivity (Wi-Fi, cellular, Bluetooth), data processing (edge/cloud computing), and user interfaces. These systems are used in smart homes, healthcare, agriculture, transportation, and industrial automation. IoT improves decision-making, efficiency, and automation by providing real-time insights and remote control. However, challenges like security, standardization, and interoperability remain critical in IoT deployments.

6. How do Cloud Computing and IoT complement each other?
Answer: Cloud Computing and IoT are closely interlinked technologies. IoT devices generate massive volumes of data, which require scalable storage and processing—capabilities offered by the cloud. Cloud platforms provide the necessary infrastructure to store, analyze, and visualize IoT data in real time. Additionally, cloud services offer APIs, machine learning tools, and dashboards that enhance IoT functionality. This synergy enables smarter applications like predictive maintenance, remote monitoring, and automated decision-making in smart cities and industries. Moreover, the cloud simplifies device management and firmware updates in large-scale IoT networks.

7. What are the major components of an IoT system?

Answer: A complete IoT system includes the following components: (1) Sensors and Actuators – capture data and interact with the environment; (2) Connectivity – facilitates data transfer (e.g., Wi-Fi, Zigbee, LTE, LoRaWAN); (3) Data Processing Unit – processes and analyzes incoming data, often using cloud or edge computing; (4) User Interface – allows users to monitor and control devices through apps or dashboards. Additionally, security, scalability, and interoperability play crucial roles in the successful deployment of IoT systems. The integration of these components enables smart operations and real-time control across various industries.

8. What are the different layers of IoT architecture?
Answer: IoT architecture typically consists of four main layers: (1) Perception Layer – includes sensors and devices that gather environmental data; (2) Network Layer – transmits data from sensors to data centers using communication protocols; (3) Processing Layer – analyzes and stores data using cloud or edge computing; (4) Application Layer – delivers services to end-users through applications such as smart homes or healthcare monitoring. Some models include additional layers like security or business layers to emphasize privacy and operational value. Understanding this layered architecture helps in designing scalable and secure IoT systems.

9. What are the challenges in IoT implementation?
Answer: IoT implementation faces several challenges: (1) Security – IoT devices are vulnerable to cyberattacks due to limited computing capabilities and poor encryption; (2) Interoperability – lack of standardization among devices and protocols; (3) Scalability – handling millions of devices and large data volumes; (4) Data Privacy – concerns about how user data is collected and used; (5) Power Management – especially in remote or battery-operated devices; (6) Network Reliability – uninterrupted connectivity is critical for real-time applications. Addressing these challenges requires a combination of robust architecture, secure design, and regulatory compliance.

10. What are the popular platforms used for Cloud-based IoT solutions?
Answer: Several cloud platforms offer integrated IoT services, including: (1) Amazon Web Services (AWS IoT Core) – supports device communication, analytics, and ML integration; (2) Microsoft Azure IoT Hub – provides device management, secure communication, and data insights; (3) Google Cloud IoT – offers scalability, real-time analytics, and AI tools; (4) IBM Watson IoT – focused on AI-powered industrial IoT solutions; (5) Oracle IoT Cloud – strong in manufacturing and logistics. These platforms provide scalable infrastructure, device SDKs, and APIs that simplify IoT development and deployment while ensuring security and reliability.

11. What is edge computing, and how does it relate to IoT?
Answer: Edge computing is a distributed computing paradigm that processes data near the source of generation, rather than relying solely on a centralized cloud. In IoT, where millions of devices produce real-time data, edge computing reduces latency, improves response times, and lowers bandwidth usage by analyzing data locally. For example, a smart factory may use edge devices to immediately detect machine failures without needing to send all data to the cloud. This decentralization is essential for time-sensitive applications like autonomous vehicles and healthcare monitoring. Edge computing enhances reliability and makes IoT systems more efficient, responsive, and scalable.

12. What is fog computing in the context of IoT?
Answer: Fog computing is an extension of cloud computing that places processing resources closer to the data sources in a network. It acts as a middle layer between IoT devices (edge) and cloud servers. While edge computing focuses on individual devices, fog computing involves routers, gateways, and servers that process and filter data within a local network before transmitting it to the cloud. This reduces latency and bandwidth usage, which is critical in time-sensitive IoT applications like traffic management or industrial control systems. Fog computing also enhances data privacy and allows faster decision-making by performing analytics locally.

13. What is the difference between cloud, fog, and edge computing?
Answer: Cloud, fog, and edge computing differ mainly in where data is processed. Cloud computing processes data in remote data centers accessible via the internet, suitable for storage and large-scale analytics. Edge computing processes data on or near the device itself, reducing latency for real-time applications. Fog computing sits between the edge and the cloud, processing data on local devices like gateways or routers. It combines the benefits of both by offering reduced latency while still allowing access to cloud resources. Choosing among these depends on application needs for speed, bandwidth, and data privacy.

14. What is SaaS in Cloud Computing?

Answer: Software as a Service (SaaS) is a cloud computing model where software applications are delivered over the internet, eliminating the need for users to install or maintain them locally. Examples include Google Workspace, Microsoft 365, and Salesforce. SaaS provides accessibility from any device with internet access, offering subscription-based pricing, automatic updates, and scalability. It benefits businesses by reducing IT infrastructure costs and simplifying software deployment. SaaS applications are hosted on remote servers, managed by the provider, and accessed via web browsers, making them ideal for email, CRM, HR, and collaboration tools.

15. What is PaaS in Cloud Computing?
Answer: Platform as a Service (PaaS) provides developers with a platform to build, test, deploy, and manage applications without managing the underlying infrastructure. It includes tools like databases, development frameworks, and operating systems. Examples include Google App Engine, Microsoft Azure App Services, and Heroku. PaaS accelerates application development by handling hosting, scaling, and maintenance, allowing developers to focus solely on coding. It supports DevOps, CI/CD pipelines, and API integration. PaaS is ideal for startups and enterprises that want to innovate rapidly without worrying about infrastructure setup and operational overhead.

16. What is IaaS in Cloud Computing?
Answer: Infrastructure as a Service (IaaS) offers fundamental computing resources such as virtual machines, storage, and networking over the cloud. It provides the building blocks for IT environments and is suitable for system administrators and IT managers. With IaaS, users control the operating systems and applications while the cloud provider manages hardware. Examples include Amazon EC2, Microsoft Azure Virtual Machines, and Google Compute Engine. IaaS is cost-effective, scalable, and flexible, enabling organizations to quickly launch new environments, run test servers, or manage disaster recovery systems with minimal upfront investment.

17. What is the importance of scalability in cloud-based IoT systems?
Answer: Scalability in cloud-based IoT systems refers to the ability to handle increasing workloads, devices, and data without degrading performance. As IoT networks grow—sometimes into millions of devices—scalable cloud infrastructure becomes essential. It allows businesses to add or reduce resources as needed, ensuring consistent service levels. Cloud platforms provide autoscaling, load balancing, and elastic storage, making it easier to manage fluctuating data loads. Scalability is crucial for real-time analytics, global deployments, and cost-efficiency. Without scalability, performance bottlenecks could lead to data loss, delayed responses, and increased operational costs in IoT ecosystems.

18. How does data analytics work in IoT using cloud computing?
Answer: Data analytics in IoT involves collecting, processing, and analyzing data from connected devices to derive insights and drive decision-making. Cloud computing supports this by offering scalable infrastructure and advanced analytics tools like machine learning and big data processing. Data collected by IoT devices is transmitted to the cloud, where services like AWS IoT Analytics or Azure Stream Analytics analyze patterns, detect anomalies, and predict trends. Real-time dashboards and reports help businesses optimize operations, forecast maintenance, and improve user experiences. The integration of analytics with IoT enables smarter, data-driven outcomes across industries.

19. What is MQTT, and why is it used in IoT?
Answer: MQTT (Message Queuing Telemetry Transport) is a lightweight messaging protocol optimized for IoT applications. It uses a publish-subscribe model to transmit data between devices and servers. MQTT is ideal for low-bandwidth, high-latency networks and constrained devices with limited power and processing capabilities. It enables reliable and efficient communication, especially in scenarios like smart homes, healthcare, and agriculture. The protocol supports Quality of Service (QoS) levels, ensuring message delivery even in unstable networks. Its simplicity and low overhead make MQTT a popular choice for IoT developers working with real-time sensor data.

20. What is CoAP in IoT, and how does it differ from MQTT?
Answer: CoAP (Constrained Application Protocol) is a lightweight protocol designed for resource-constrained IoT devices and networks. Unlike MQTT's publish-subscribe model, CoAP follows a request-response model similar to HTTP. It operates over UDP (User Datagram Protocol), making it faster but less reliable compared to TCP-based MQTT. CoAP is ideal for applications that require low overhead and can tolerate some data loss, such as environmental monitoring. It supports multicast, low header size, and asynchronous communication. While MQTT is better for continuous data streaming, CoAP is suitable for RESTful interactions and sensor data polling in constrained environments.

21. What is the role of sensors in an IoT ecosystem?
Answer: Sensors are crucial components of the IoT ecosystem, responsible for collecting real-world data such as temperature, pressure, humidity, motion, and light. They serve as the "eyes and ears" of IoT devices, enabling them to interact with their environment. This data is transmitted to processing units for analysis, decision-making, or remote control. In smart homes, for example, temperature sensors help automate heating systems. In agriculture, soil moisture sensors assist in irrigation management. The accuracy, efficiency, and placement of sensors significantly impact the effectiveness of IoT applications across all industries.

22. How does cloud computing enhance data security in IoT applications?
Answer: Cloud computing enhances data security in IoT applications by offering centralized control, data encryption, secure access controls, and compliance with global standards. Leading cloud providers implement multi-layered security protocols including SSL/TLS encryption, identity and access management (IAM), intrusion detection, and DDoS protection. Cloud platforms also enable regular security updates and patches, minimizing vulnerabilities. In addition, tools like audit logs, token-based access, and anomaly detection help monitor suspicious activities. By leveraging cloud security best practices, IoT developers can ensure device data is protected from unauthorized access and breaches.

23. What is the importance of API in IoT and cloud integration?
Answer: APIs (Application Programming Interfaces) are essential for connecting IoT devices to cloud platforms. They enable seamless data exchange, device control, and integration with third-party services. APIs allow developers to send and receive data between sensors and cloud applications, facilitating tasks like data visualization, remote monitoring, and automation. RESTful APIs are commonly used due to their simplicity and compatibility with HTTP. APIs also help in device provisioning, firmware updates, and analytics integration. In essence, APIs act as a bridge between IoT hardware and cloud software, enabling scalable, interoperable, and real-time applications.

24. What is a digital twin in IoT?
Answer: A digital twin is a virtual replica of a physical object, system, or process that uses real-time data collected from IoT devices to mirror the behavior and performance of its physical counterpart. It enables simulation, monitoring, and optimization without interacting with the actual asset. For example, a digital twin of a wind turbine can predict wear and optimize maintenance schedules. Cloud platforms host digital twin models and provide analytics and AI integration. Digital twins enhance predictive maintenance, reduce downtime, and improve design and operational efficiency across industries like manufacturing, healthcare, and smart cities.

25. What is serverless computing in the context of IoT?
Answer: Serverless computing allows developers to run backend code without managing or provisioning servers. In IoT, it enables lightweight and scalable execution of data processing, event handling, or automation logic. Services like AWS Lambda and Azure Functions trigger code execution in response to IoT events such as device messages or alarms. Serverless architectures reduce infrastructure costs and allow auto-scaling, which is ideal for sporadic workloads. It simplifies development and lets teams focus on application logic rather than server maintenance, making it an efficient model for real-time IoT data processing and control.

26. What is cloud orchestration in IoT?
Answer: Cloud orchestration refers to the automated coordination, arrangement, and management of cloud services and resources to optimize workflows and data processes. In the context of IoT, orchestration helps manage device connectivity, data routing, security, storage, and processing across cloud environments. It ensures that services like data ingestion, real-time analytics, and alerts work together seamlessly. Orchestration tools also automate the deployment and scaling of applications, helping IoT solutions remain efficient and responsive. Platforms like Kubernetes or Azure IoT Hub offer orchestration capabilities. This concept is vital for reducing human error, ensuring consistency, and handling complex IoT ecosystems at scale.

27. What is a cloud service model and why is it important in IoT?
Answer: A cloud service model defines the level of service abstraction provided by cloud providers. The three main models—SaaS, PaaS, and IaaS—offer flexibility for different IoT use cases. IaaS provides raw infrastructure for hosting applications and storing IoT data. PaaS offers a development environment to build IoT apps without managing hardware. SaaS delivers ready-to-use tools for analytics or device monitoring. Choosing the right service model

impacts cost, scalability, control, and ease of development. In IoT, the appropriate service model ensures efficient device integration, data handling, and application deployment, making it critical to overall system success.

28. What are IoT platforms and give examples?
Answer: IoT platforms are integrated services that support the development, management, and deployment of IoT applications. They provide tools for device management, data collection, analytics, and connectivity. Common features include real-time data visualization, cloud integration, and API access. Examples include AWS IoT Core, Google Cloud IoT, Microsoft Azure IoT Hub, IBM Watson IoT, and ThingSpeak. These platforms simplify IoT project implementation by offering pre-built infrastructure and services, reducing time-to-market and development cost. They also provide scalability and security, making them ideal for both startups and enterprises to build robust IoT ecosystems.

29. What is virtualization and how is it used in cloud computing for IoT?
Answer: Virtualization is the creation of virtual instances of hardware, software, storage, or network resources. In cloud computing, it enables multiple virtual machines (VMs) to run on a single physical server, maximizing resource utilization and efficiency. For IoT, virtualization allows flexible scaling, testing, and deployment of applications without needing physical servers. It enables edge gateways and cloud servers to run virtual instances for managing IoT traffic, analytics, or simulation environments. Technologies like hypervisors and containers (e.g., Docker) help isolate workloads. Virtualization is essential for rapid deployment, cost control, and resource optimization in cloud-based IoT infrastructures.

30. What is containerization in cloud and IoT?
Answer: Containerization is the practice of packaging applications and their dependencies into lightweight, portable units called containers. Unlike traditional virtual machines, containers share the host OS kernel, making them faster and more efficient. In cloud and IoT, containers are used to deploy microservices and applications across edge devices and cloud environments seamlessly. Tools like Docker and orchestration systems like Kubernetes are widely used. Containers enable consistent environments, faster deployment, scalability, and easier updates. In IoT, this is particularly valuable for managing software across a large number of heterogeneous devices with minimal overhead.

31. What is a gateway in IoT architecture?
Answer: A gateway in IoT serves as a bridge between IoT devices and cloud services. It collects data from sensors and devices using protocols like Zigbee, Bluetooth, or LoRaWAN, and then transmits it to the cloud over Wi-Fi, Ethernet, or cellular networks. The gateway may also preprocess data, apply security checks, and manage device connectivity. It plays a crucial role in filtering, aggregating, and securing data before cloud ingestion. In industrial environments, gateways enhance reliability by ensuring continuous operation even when internet connectivity is unstable. They are key to ensuring interoperability and efficient communication in large IoT systems.

32. What is load balancing in cloud computing?
Answer: Load balancing is the process of distributing workloads evenly across multiple computing resources, such as servers or virtual machines. In cloud computing, it ensures high availability, fault tolerance, and efficient use of resources. For IoT systems, where millions of devices may generate data simultaneously, load balancers prevent any single server from being overwhelmed. They automatically reroute traffic based on resource usage and availability, ensuring continuous performance and minimizing downtime. Cloud providers offer load balancing as a service (e.g., AWS Elastic Load Balancer, Azure Load Balancer) to support scalable and responsive IoT applications.

33. What is latency and why is it important in IoT?
Answer: Latency refers to the delay between the transmission and receipt of data. In IoT systems, low latency is critical for real-time applications like autonomous driving, health monitoring, or industrial automation, where delays can result in failures or hazards. Factors affecting latency include network bandwidth, processing speed, and distance between devices and servers. Edge computing and 5G technology are being adopted to minimize latency by processing data closer to the source. Understanding and optimizing latency is essential for building responsive, efficient, and safe IoT systems, especially in mission-critical scenarios.

34. What is 5G and how does it impact IoT and cloud computing?
Answer: 5G is the fifth generation of wireless communication technology, offering high-speed data transfer, ultra-low latency, and massive device connectivity. For IoT, 5G enables real-time communication, supporting applications like

smart cities, autonomous vehicles, and remote surgeries. It enhances cloud computing by providing faster, more reliable connections between IoT devices and cloud platforms. The increased bandwidth allows seamless video streaming, faster firmware updates, and improved responsiveness. 5G also supports network slicing, allowing customized network environments for specific IoT use cases. Its introduction is transforming the scalability, reliability, and capabilities of IoT-cloud ecosystems.

35. What is big data analytics in IoT?

Answer: Big data analytics in IoT involves processing large volumes of structured and unstructured data generated by connected devices to extract actionable insights. This includes real-time and batch analytics for anomaly detection, trend prediction, and performance optimization. Cloud platforms like AWS, Azure, and Google Cloud provide scalable tools to ingest, store, and analyze IoT data. Big data frameworks like Hadoop, Spark, and Flink are also used. By analyzing IoT data, businesses can optimize operations, enhance user experiences, and make informed decisions. Big data analytics is fundamental to unlocking the value of IoT deployments.

36. What are smart devices in IoT?

Answer: Smart devices are embedded systems with sensors, actuators, and communication capabilities that collect and exchange data over networks. Examples include smart thermostats, fitness trackers, smart bulbs, and industrial sensors. These devices are key components of the IoT ecosystem and rely on cloud platforms for data storage, analytics, and remote control. Smart devices operate autonomously or in coordination with other devices to perform tasks, monitor conditions, or trigger actions. They are central to smart homes, healthcare, agriculture, and industrial automation. Their functionality, interoperability, and connectivity define the intelligence and efficiency of IoT systems.

37. What is real-time processing in IoT and cloud?

Answer: Real-time processing in IoT refers to the immediate analysis and response to data as it is generated by devices. In cloud computing, this is achieved using stream processing tools like Apache Kafka, AWS Kinesis, and Azure Stream Analytics. Real-time processing enables applications like fraud detection, predictive maintenance, and emergency alerts. For instance, a temperature sensor in a cold storage facility can instantly trigger an alert if thresholds are breached. Real-time capabilities are essential for safety, efficiency, and user experience in dynamic environments, and are increasingly supported by cloud-edge hybrid architectures.

38. What are IoT security best practices in the cloud?

Answer: IoT security best practices in the cloud include encryption of data in transit and at rest, device authentication, secure APIs, regular patching, and access control mechanisms. Network segmentation, intrusion detection systems, and anomaly monitoring are also essential. Using cloud security tools such as IAM (Identity and Access Management), token-based authentication, and SSL/TLS protocols helps protect against unauthorized access. Organizations should also conduct regular security audits, firmware updates, and vulnerability assessments. These measures ensure the confidentiality, integrity, and availability of data, which are critical for maintaining trust in IoT-cloud infrastructures.

39. What is device provisioning in IoT?

Answer: Device provisioning is the process of configuring and onboarding new IoT devices to a network so they can communicate securely and effectively with cloud services. This includes assigning device identities, installing certificates or keys, configuring network settings, and registering with cloud platforms. Automated provisioning tools like AWS IoT Device Management or Azure DPS simplify this task at scale. Proper provisioning ensures secure connectivity, simplifies updates, and supports lifecycle management. It is a vital step in maintaining large IoT deployments, reducing manual intervention, and ensuring consistent configurations across all connected devices.

40. What is multi-tenancy in cloud computing?

Answer: Multi-tenancy is a cloud computing architecture where a single instance of a software application serves multiple customers (tenants), with data isolation and secure access controls. This model optimizes resource usage, reduces operational costs, and enables scalability. In IoT, multi-tenancy allows service providers to support multiple clients using a single platform, each with their own set of devices, data, and dashboards. It simplifies infrastructure management while maintaining performance and security boundaries. Proper multi-tenancy implementation is crucial for SaaS-based IoT applications, particularly those serving various customers or regions from a centralized cloud environment.

41. What are actuators in IoT systems?
Answer: Actuators are devices in an IoT system that convert electrical signals into physical actions. They receive commands from controllers or cloud platforms and perform tasks such as opening a valve, rotating a motor, or adjusting temperature. Actuators work alongside sensors, which collect environmental data. In a smart irrigation system, for example, a sensor detects soil dryness, and an actuator turns on the water supply. Actuators are critical for automation and remote control in IoT applications across manufacturing, agriculture, smart homes, and more. They bring intelligence to physical systems by enabling real-time interactions with the environment.

42. What is a REST API in IoT-cloud communication?
Answer: A REST API (Representational State Transfer Application Programming Interface) is a web-based communication method that allows IoT devices and applications to exchange data using standard HTTP methods. REST APIs are lightweight, easy to implement, and widely supported, making them ideal for cloud integration in IoT. Devices can use REST to send data to cloud servers, retrieve configurations, or control actuators. JSON is typically used for data formatting. RESTful APIs promote interoperability, scalability, and stateless communication, which simplifies development and enhances reliability in IoT-cloud ecosystems.

43. What are some challenges in integrating IoT with cloud computing?
Answer: Challenges in integrating IoT with cloud computing include data security and privacy concerns, latency issues, managing massive data volumes, device heterogeneity, and connectivity reliability. Interoperability between various hardware and software standards can hinder integration. Power constraints and limited processing capabilities of edge devices also pose challenges. Additionally, compliance with regulations like GDPR and data sovereignty laws must be considered when transmitting data across borders. Overcoming these challenges requires robust architecture, hybrid models (cloud-edge), strong encryption, scalable infrastructure, and continuous monitoring.

44. What is interoperability in IoT?
Answer: Interoperability in IoT refers to the ability of different devices, platforms, and systems to communicate and work together effectively. It ensures seamless data exchange and collaboration between heterogeneous components regardless of manufacturer or protocol. This is critical for building scalable and flexible IoT ecosystems. Standards like MQTT, CoAP, and REST APIs enhance interoperability. Without it, system integration becomes complex and costly. Interoperability supports innovation, reduces vendor lock-in, and allows users to combine various technologies for customized solutions in smart homes, healthcare, and industrial automation.

45. What is a data lake and its role in IoT?
Answer: A data lake is a centralized repository that stores vast amounts of raw data in its native format, including structured, semi-structured, and unstructured data. In IoT, it collects sensor readings, logs, images, and real-time streams from diverse sources. Cloud-based data lakes like AWS S3 or Azure Data Lake enable cost-effective storage and flexible analytics. They support machine learning, big data analytics, and visualization. Data lakes are vital for deriving insights, training predictive models, and supporting decision-making in IoT applications across industries.

46. What is telemetry in IoT?
Answer: Telemetry in IoT refers to the automatic collection and transmission of data from remote devices to a central system, typically over cloud infrastructure. It involves monitoring parameters such as temperature, pressure, location, or performance metrics. Telemetry enables real-time tracking, diagnostics, and predictive maintenance. In automotive IoT, for instance, telemetry data informs manufacturers about engine performance or fault conditions. Cloud platforms store, analyze, and visualize telemetry data to improve efficiency, ensure safety, and support proactive interventions in various IoT domains.

47. What is device shadowing in cloud IoT platforms?
Answer: Device shadowing is a technique used in cloud IoT platforms to maintain a virtual representation of a physical device's state. It stores desired, reported, and metadata states, allowing applications to interact with devices even when offline. For example, AWS IoT uses device shadows to update thermostat settings while the device is temporarily disconnected. When the device reconnects, it synchronizes with its shadow. This improves reliability, supports offline operations, and simplifies state management. Device shadows ensure consistency and enhance user experience in large-scale IoT deployments.

48. What is an IoT dashboard and how is it used?

Answer: An IoT dashboard is a visual interface that displays real-time data, analytics, and control options for IoT devices and systems. It allows users to monitor performance, set alerts, and manage devices through charts, maps, or gauges. Dashboards are typically hosted on cloud platforms and are customizable. They provide actionable insights for users in sectors like smart cities, agriculture, and industrial monitoring. A well-designed dashboard simplifies complex data and supports quick decision-making, contributing to better efficiency, automation, and visibility in IoT operations.

49. What is firmware over-the-air (FOTA) in IoT?
Answer: Firmware Over-The-Air (FOTA) is the process of remotely updating the firmware of IoT devices via cloud services. It allows manufacturers and operators to fix bugs, add features, or patch vulnerabilities without physical access. FOTA reduces maintenance costs, enhances device security, and improves user experience. It is commonly used in smartphones, smart appliances, and automotive systems. Secure delivery mechanisms, validation checks, and rollback options are essential to prevent failures. FOTA ensures that large fleets of devices remain up-to-date and functional with minimal downtime.

50. What is cloud-native IoT architecture?
Answer: Cloud-native IoT architecture refers to designing IoT applications specifically to leverage the advantages of cloud environments, including scalability, automation, and resilience. It utilizes microservices, containers, serverless functions, and APIs to build modular and distributed systems. This architecture supports continuous integration and deployment, real-time data handling, and flexible resource allocation. Cloud-native design ensures better fault tolerance, scalability, and rapid innovation. It aligns with DevOps and agile practices, making it ideal for dynamic IoT ecosystems that need to scale quickly and adapt to changing user needs or market conditions.

51. What is cloud-native computing and how does it relate to IoT?
Answer: Cloud-native computing is a design approach that builds and runs scalable applications in modern cloud environments using containers, microservices, dynamic orchestration, and continuous delivery. In the IoT domain, cloud-native practices allow developers to deploy scalable, resilient, and modular IoT applications. With millions of devices generating real-time data, cloud-native applications ensure better handling of distributed workloads. Kubernetes, Docker, and serverless functions allow quick updates and easier integration. This approach also supports agile development and improves time-to-market for IoT products by leveraging cloud capabilities such as scalability, elasticity, and fault tolerance.

52. What is edge analytics and how is it useful in IoT?
Answer: Edge analytics is the process of collecting and analyzing data at the edge of the network—close to the data source—rather than transmitting it all to a central cloud server. In IoT, it is especially useful when low latency, real-time decision-making, or bandwidth savings are required. For example, in autonomous vehicles or industrial automation, edge analytics can process sensor data instantly to trigger actions. This approach reduces cloud dependency, enhances speed, and lowers data transmission costs. Edge devices like Raspberry Pi, NVIDIA Jetson, or specialized gateways often perform such localized processing.

53. How does fog computing differ from edge computing in IoT?
Answer: While both fog and edge computing bring computation closer to the source, they differ in architecture. Edge computing processes data directly on the device or nearby edge nodes, offering ultra-low latency. Fog computing introduces an intermediate layer between the edge and the cloud—often called "fog nodes"—that perform preprocessing before forwarding relevant data to the cloud. Fog computing supports scenarios where multiple edge devices need coordination or where regulatory or bandwidth constraints exist. It is commonly used in smart cities and industrial IoT where complex, real-time analytics and control are required across many distributed nodes.

54. What is a mesh network and its application in IoT?
Answer: A mesh network is a decentralized network topology where each device (or node) connects directly and dynamically with others, forming a web-like structure. In IoT, mesh networks are used to ensure reliable, self-healing communication, especially in environments where internet access is limited or unreliable. Zigbee and Thread are popular mesh protocols. Mesh networks are useful in home automation, agriculture, and industrial IoT settings. Their advantages include redundancy, scalability, and better coverage without relying on a central hub. If one node fails, data is rerouted through another, ensuring continuous operation.

55. What is MQTT and why is it preferred in IoT communication?
Answer: MQTT (Message Queuing Telemetry Transport) is a lightweight messaging protocol based on the publish-subscribe model, designed for low-bandwidth and unreliable networks. It is ideal for IoT because it requires minimal power, supports small payloads, and maintains real-time bi-directional communication. Devices publish messages to topics, and subscribers receive only the messages of interest. MQTT is used in home automation, telemetry, and mobile applications. It ensures efficient device-to-cloud communication, even in constrained environments. Its simplicity, low overhead, and scalability make it the preferred protocol for many IoT systems.

56. What is CoAP and how does it support IoT devices?
Answer: CoAP (Constrained Application Protocol) is a web transfer protocol similar to HTTP but optimized for constrained devices and networks, typically found in IoT environments. It operates over UDP, ensuring minimal overhead and faster performance compared to TCP. CoAP enables RESTful interaction (GET, POST, PUT, DELETE) with low-power devices like sensors and actuators. It supports asynchronous communication, multicast requests, and is designed to work efficiently in low-bandwidth, high-latency conditions. CoAP is widely used in smart energy systems, smart homes, and wearable devices due to its simplicity and efficiency.

57. What is a smart grid and how does IoT enhance it?
Answer: A smart grid is an advanced electricity network that uses digital technology and IoT to monitor, manage, and optimize the generation, distribution, and consumption of electricity. IoT devices like smart meters, sensors, and automated switches collect and share data in real-time, enabling demand forecasting, fault detection, and load balancing. This helps reduce energy waste, enhances reliability, and supports renewable energy integration. Consumers can monitor usage and adjust behavior through IoT-powered apps. The smart grid improves grid efficiency, reduces costs, and supports a sustainable energy future.

58. What are LPWAN technologies and their role in IoT?
Answer: Low Power Wide Area Network (LPWAN) technologies like LoRaWAN, NB-IoT, and Sigfox are designed for long-range communication with minimal power consumption. These are ideal for IoT applications requiring long battery life and remote connectivity, such as smart agriculture, logistics tracking, and environmental monitoring. LPWANs typically support low data rates and are not suitable for high-bandwidth use cases. Their ability to connect thousands of devices over kilometers with low energy use makes them vital in massive IoT deployments, especially in rural or industrial settings.

59. What are IoT protocols and why are they important?
Answer: IoT protocols are communication standards that enable data exchange between devices and systems. Common protocols include MQTT, CoAP, HTTP, Bluetooth, Zigbee, and LoRaWAN. These protocols address different layers—network, transport, and application—ensuring reliable and secure communication. Choosing the right protocol depends on use-case requirements like data rate, range, power consumption, and latency. Protocols are essential for ensuring interoperability, data integrity, and efficient resource use in IoT networks. Without standardized protocols, integrating devices from multiple vendors would be challenging.

60. What is IoT architecture and its main layers?
Answer: IoT architecture defines the structure of an IoT system and typically includes four main layers:
1. Perception Layer: Contains sensors and actuators that interact with the environment.
2. Network Layer: Transmits data to cloud or edge servers.
3. Processing Layer: Analyzes and stores data, often via cloud platforms.
4. Application Layer: Interfaces with users through dashboards or apps.

This layered approach helps in designing scalable, modular, and secure systems. Each layer has specific roles, enabling the smooth functioning of complex IoT ecosystems such as smart cities or industrial automation platforms.

61. How does IoT impact healthcare systems?
Answer: IoT revolutionizes healthcare by enabling remote patient monitoring, real-time diagnostics, and personalized treatment. Wearables like fitness trackers, ECG monitors, and glucose sensors collect health data, which is transmitted to cloud-based systems for analysis. Doctors can remotely track patient vitals and receive alerts during emergencies. IoT also supports hospital asset tracking, smart beds, and automated medication dispensers. It improves healthcare access, reduces costs, and enhances patient outcomes. However, security, data privacy, and regulatory compliance (like HIPAA) must be ensured for safe IoT deployment in healthcare.

62. What is predictive maintenance in IoT?
Answer: Predictive maintenance uses IoT sensors and analytics to predict equipment failures before they occur. Devices continuously monitor parameters like temperature, vibration, and pressure. The collected data is analyzed using cloud-based machine learning algorithms to identify patterns that precede failures. This allows maintenance to be performed just in time—avoiding unnecessary downtime or over-servicing. Industries like manufacturing, aviation, and energy benefit greatly from predictive maintenance. It improves operational efficiency, reduces repair costs, and prolongs equipment life, making it a major application of IoT in industry.

63. What is smart agriculture and how does IoT support it?
Answer: Smart agriculture uses IoT technologies to monitor and optimize farming operations. Sensors track soil moisture, temperature, humidity, and crop health. Automated irrigation systems adjust water usage based on sensor input, improving resource use. Drones and GPS-enabled equipment collect aerial and ground data, aiding in precision farming. Farmers can access real-time insights via cloud dashboards. IoT in agriculture improves yield, reduces waste, and supports sustainable practices. It is especially beneficial in regions facing water scarcity or climate variability.

64. What is a digital twin and its role in IoT?
Answer: A digital twin is a virtual representation of a physical object or system, continuously updated with real-time IoT data. It mirrors the physical asset's condition, behavior, and performance. Digital twins are used in manufacturing, aerospace, and smart cities to simulate operations, predict issues, and plan maintenance. Cloud platforms host and manage these digital models. They allow remote monitoring, testing scenarios without risk, and improving efficiency. Digital twins enhance decision-making, reduce downtime, and help in building resilient IoT-enabled systems.

65. What is an IoT gateway and what are its features?
Answer: An IoT gateway acts as a bridge between edge devices and the cloud. It aggregates data from sensors, performs local processing or filtering, and transmits relevant data to cloud platforms. Features include protocol translation, data buffering, encryption, and sometimes AI-based analytics. Gateways reduce cloud load, improve response time, and enhance security. They are especially useful in remote locations where constant internet connectivity is not guaranteed. Gateways are critical in industrial IoT, smart buildings, and vehicular networks.

66. What is serverless computing and how does it help IoT?
Answer: Serverless computing allows developers to run code without managing servers. In IoT, serverless platforms (like AWS Lambda or Azure Functions) handle event-driven tasks—such as responding to sensor input or triggering alerts—automatically. It reduces operational overhead, supports scalability, and lowers cost since billing is based on execution time. Serverless architecture simplifies IoT development, making it ideal for small, frequent workloads like data validation, filtering, or processing triggered by IoT device events.

67. What is multi-cloud strategy in IoT?
Answer: A multi-cloud strategy uses services from multiple cloud providers (e.g., AWS, Azure, GCP) to avoid vendor lock-in, improve resilience, and optimize performance or cost. In IoT, multi-cloud allows developers to store data in different regions, use specific services from different vendors, or ensure redundancy. It improves flexibility and ensures that critical IoT operations are not tied to one platform. However, managing multi-cloud systems requires robust monitoring, security, and integration tools.

68. How does AI complement IoT in cloud computing?
Answer: Artificial Intelligence enhances IoT by analyzing vast sensor data to detect patterns, predict outcomes, and automate responses. AI models are deployed in the cloud to process IoT-generated data for tasks like image recognition, anomaly detection, or predictive maintenance. For example, AI-powered smart cameras can identify security threats in real-time. Integration of AI with IoT enables intelligent automation, adaptive systems, and better decision-making. This combination, often called AIoT (Artificial Intelligence of Things), transforms industries by adding learning and intelligence to connected systems.

69. What is a smart city and how is IoT involved?
Answer: A smart city uses IoT technologies to enhance urban infrastructure, services, and quality of life. Connected sensors and devices collect data on traffic, air quality, energy usage, and public safety. This data is analyzed on cloud platforms to optimize resource usage, reduce pollution, and improve citizen services. Applications include smart

lighting, intelligent traffic systems, waste management, and emergency response. IoT helps cities become more sustainable, efficient, and citizen-friendly by enabling data-driven governance and automation.

70. What is data ingestion in cloud IoT systems?
Answer: Data ingestion is the process of collecting, importing, and processing real-time or batch data from IoT devices into cloud systems. Tools like AWS Kinesis, Azure Event Hubs, or Apache Kafka handle high-speed ingestion of data from millions of devices. The ingested data is stored, analyzed, or visualized for further insights. Efficient ingestion ensures minimal data loss, fast processing, and reliable analytics. It is a key component of IoT architecture, enabling real-time decision-making and system automation.

71. What are the main components of an IoT ecosystem?
Answer: An IoT ecosystem is a complex network composed of several integral components working together to collect, transmit, process, and act on data. The main components include sensors/devices, which gather data from the environment; connectivity modules, like Wi-Fi, Bluetooth, or Zigbee, which transmit the data; data processing units, often located in the cloud or edge devices; and a user interface to monitor or control the system. Additionally, a data storage system and security layer are essential to protect data integrity and privacy. These elements together create a robust IoT ecosystem that supports automation, remote monitoring, and intelligent decision-making.

72. What is the role of fog computing in IoT?
Answer: Fog computing acts as an intermediary layer between IoT devices and the cloud, bringing computation and storage closer to the data source. In IoT, real-time processing is often critical, and sending every data point to the cloud introduces latency. Fog computing reduces this delay by processing data at or near the edge of the network. This improves response time, saves bandwidth, and enhances privacy. It is particularly useful in scenarios like industrial automation, healthcare, and smart cities, where decisions must be made in milliseconds. Fog computing, therefore, supports IoT by enhancing speed, efficiency, and scalability.

73. How does data security impact cloud-based IoT systems?
Answer: Data security is a crucial concern in cloud-based IoT systems due to the massive volumes of sensitive data being transmitted and stored. IoT devices often have limited processing capabilities, making them vulnerable to attacks. When integrated with the cloud, any breach in the cloud infrastructure could expose user data or allow unauthorized control over devices. Security measures like encryption, secure communication protocols (HTTPS, MQTT with TLS), regular firmware updates, authentication, and access control are vital. Cloud providers must also comply with data protection laws and offer advanced security frameworks. Poor security undermines user trust and may lead to legal consequences.

74. What are cloud-native applications, and how do they relate to IoT?
Answer: Cloud-native applications are designed specifically for cloud environments using microservices, containers, and dynamic orchestration tools like Kubernetes. These applications are highly scalable, resilient, and adaptable to change. In the context of IoT, cloud-native architectures support the scalability required for millions of connected devices. IoT systems generate large volumes of data that need to be processed in real-time, and cloud-native solutions facilitate this with elastic resources. Furthermore, microservices architecture allows developers to update or scale parts of the system independently. This makes cloud-native applications ideal for managing complex, distributed IoT networks efficiently.

75. What is the significance of REST APIs in IoT and cloud integration?
Answer: REST (Representational State Transfer) APIs are widely used in IoT and cloud integration for facilitating communication between devices and cloud services. REST APIs use standard HTTP methods, making them lightweight and easy to implement across various platforms and devices. In IoT, REST APIs allow devices to send data to cloud platforms for storage, processing, or further action. They also enable remote configuration, monitoring, and device control. Their stateless nature ensures scalability and robustness, which are crucial in cloud-IoT systems. RESTful APIs thus act as the backbone of many IoT ecosystems, enabling interoperability and seamless data flow.

76. How does 5G technology enhance IoT applications?
Answer: 5G technology significantly enhances IoT applications by offering higher bandwidth, ultra-low latency, and increased device connectivity. These capabilities are critical for time-sensitive applications such as autonomous vehicles, remote surgeries, and industrial automation. Unlike its predecessors, 5G supports massive machine-type

communications (mMTC), allowing thousands of devices to connect per square kilometer without network congestion. It also facilitates real-time data processing, which is essential for responsive IoT systems. The enhanced capabilities of 5G open new possibilities for smart cities, connected healthcare, and intelligent transportation systems, enabling faster, more reliable, and more scalable IoT deployments.

77. What is the importance of virtualization in cloud computing?
Answer: Virtualization is a foundational technology in cloud computing that allows multiple virtual instances of computing environments to run on a single physical machine. It enables better utilization of hardware resources, reduces operational costs, and increases system flexibility. For cloud providers, virtualization allows efficient workload distribution and scalability. For users, it offers the ability to deploy virtual machines quickly, run different operating systems, and ensure application isolation. In the IoT context, virtualization supports testing, development, and deployment of applications across varied environments without the need for dedicated physical hardware.

78. What is multi-tenancy in cloud computing?
Answer: Multi-tenancy is a cloud computing architecture where a single software instance serves multiple customers (tenants). Each tenant's data and configuration are isolated, but the underlying infrastructure and application code are shared. This model improves resource utilization and reduces operational costs for cloud providers. For IoT applications, multi-tenancy is beneficial as it allows multiple organizations to use the same IoT platform securely and independently. It ensures scalability, cost-effectiveness, and efficient maintenance. However, it also necessitates robust security mechanisms to prevent data leakage and ensure privacy across tenants.

79. What are the types of cloud storage used in IoT systems?
Answer: Cloud storage in IoT systems is essential for storing vast amounts of data generated by sensors and devices. The main types include object storage, file storage, and block storage. Object storage is ideal for unstructured data and provides scalability and durability, commonly used in applications like video surveillance. File storage allows access to data using standard file protocols, suitable for collaborative environments. Block storage is used for databases and high-performance applications requiring low latency. Each storage type serves different purposes in an IoT architecture, and often, a combination is used depending on the system's needs.

80. How is MQTT used in IoT communication?
Answer: MQTT (Message Queuing Telemetry Transport) is a lightweight messaging protocol designed for constrained devices and low-bandwidth, high-latency networks, making it ideal for IoT. It operates on a publish/subscribe model, where devices (clients) publish data to topics, and others subscribe to receive that data. MQTT ensures minimal overhead, energy efficiency, and real-time data exchange. It is widely used in smart homes, industrial IoT, and healthcare devices. MQTT's simplicity, low power usage, and support for asynchronous communication make it a preferred choice for reliable and scalable IoT deployments.

81. What is the role of edge computing in IoT systems?
Answer: Edge computing brings data processing closer to the location where it is generated, reducing the need to transfer vast amounts of data to centralized cloud servers. In IoT systems, where devices constantly generate real-time data, edge computing enables faster responses, lowers latency, and reduces bandwidth usage. For instance, in smart manufacturing or autonomous vehicles, edge computing can process data instantly, allowing immediate actions without waiting for cloud-based instructions. It also helps enhance data privacy since sensitive data can be processed locally. Ultimately, edge computing improves the efficiency, speed, and scalability of IoT deployments.

82. How does cloud computing support data analytics in IoT?
Answer: Cloud computing provides scalable infrastructure and powerful tools for processing and analyzing vast amounts of data generated by IoT devices. It enables real-time analytics using services like AWS IoT Analytics, Google Cloud IoT Core, or Azure IoT Hub. These platforms offer machine learning models, big data pipelines, and visualization tools that help convert raw sensor data into actionable insights. Cloud-based analytics help identify trends, predict failures, and optimize operations. It allows IoT systems to make intelligent decisions, supports predictive maintenance, and improves customer experience through data-driven strategies.

83. What is CoAP and how is it used in IoT?
Answer: CoAP (Constrained Application Protocol) is a lightweight protocol designed for resource-constrained IoT devices and networks. It is based on the REST model and works over UDP, offering features like low overhead,

multicast support, and asynchronous communication. CoAP is ideal for low-power wireless networks like 6LoWPAN. It enables devices such as sensors and actuators to communicate efficiently with servers and applications. Unlike HTTP, CoAP is optimized for energy and bandwidth savings, making it suitable for smart cities, environmental monitoring, and home automation. It also supports built-in reliability mechanisms through message acknowledgment and retransmission.

84. What is cloud orchestration in IoT architecture?
Answer: Cloud orchestration in IoT refers to the automated coordination and management of various cloud services and IoT resources. It includes deploying applications, managing workloads, scaling resources, and ensuring service dependencies are maintained. Orchestration tools such as Kubernetes or AWS CloudFormation simplify the complexity of managing thousands of devices and cloud-based applications. In IoT, orchestration ensures seamless operation by automating updates, resource allocation, fault recovery, and device provisioning. It increases operational efficiency, reduces manual intervention, and helps maintain consistency across diverse environments.

85. What is the significance of APIs in cloud-IoT integration?
Answer: APIs (Application Programming Interfaces) are essential in integrating IoT devices with cloud platforms. They enable communication between sensors, gateways, and cloud services by providing standard protocols for data exchange and control. RESTful and MQTT APIs allow developers to read sensor data, control actuators, and access cloud analytics. APIs promote modular design, interoperability, and scalability. In a multi-device environment, APIs simplify development, enhance flexibility, and support third-party integration. They are crucial for creating smart ecosystems, such as smart homes or industrial automation, where various components must work together seamlessly.

86. What are the key differences between IoT and M2M communication?
Answer: While both IoT (Internet of Things) and M2M (Machine-to-Machine) involve machine communication, their scope and technology differ. M2M is typically point-to-point and uses private networks like cellular or RF, focusing on direct device communication. IoT, on the other hand, integrates devices into the internet, allowing remote monitoring, data analytics, and cloud-based control. IoT systems are more scalable and involve web protocols, cloud computing, and big data analysis. While M2M suits simple automation tasks, IoT enables complex, intelligent ecosystems with broader connectivity and data insights.

87. What is the importance of scalability in cloud-based IoT platforms?
Answer: Scalability refers to a system's ability to handle increasing amounts of work or add resources without performance loss. In cloud-based IoT platforms, scalability is vital as the number of connected devices and data volume can grow exponentially. Cloud providers offer elastic computing resources, allowing organizations to scale infrastructure up or down based on demand. This flexibility prevents system overload, reduces costs, and supports long-term growth. Scalable IoT platforms ensure consistent performance, efficient data processing, and user satisfaction even under high traffic or during system expansion.

88. What is the difference between cloud computing and grid computing?
Answer: Cloud computing and grid computing both involve distributed computing resources, but they differ in structure and purpose. Cloud computing offers on-demand, scalable services through virtualization and is managed by providers like AWS or Azure. It supports pay-as-you-go models and is ideal for IoT, web apps, and enterprise services. Grid computing, however, connects multiple computing systems across locations to solve large-scale computational problems. It's commonly used in research and scientific simulations. While cloud computing emphasizes service delivery, grid computing focuses on collaborative computation using shared resources.

89. What is a digital twin and how is it used in IoT?
Answer: A digital twin is a virtual replica of a physical object, system, or process, continuously updated with real-time data from IoT devices. It enables monitoring, simulation, and prediction of behavior without interacting with the actual object. In industries like manufacturing, healthcare, and smart cities, digital twins improve performance, reduce downtime, and optimize maintenance. For example, a digital twin of a jet engine allows engineers to analyze wear patterns and predict failures. Powered by IoT and cloud analytics, digital twins revolutionize design, testing, and operations across sectors.

90. What is serverless computing in the context of IoT?

Answer: Serverless computing allows developers to build and run applications without managing the underlying infrastructure. In IoT, it enables event-driven processing where cloud functions are triggered by device actions, such as sending data or receiving a command. Serverless platforms like AWS Lambda or Azure Functions automatically scale based on the number of events. This model reduces operational complexity, saves costs, and supports real-time processing. It is ideal for applications requiring high scalability and sporadic workloads, such as smart home automation or environmental monitoring systems.

91. What is latency and why is it critical in IoT applications?
Answer: Latency refers to the delay between a data request and its response. In IoT, low latency is critical for applications requiring real-time or near-real-time responses, such as autonomous vehicles, remote surgeries, and industrial control systems. High latency can lead to delayed actions, safety hazards, or performance degradation. To reduce latency, edge computing is often used alongside cloud services. Network optimization, lightweight protocols like MQTT, and dedicated bandwidth also help. Managing latency is key to ensuring the reliability and effectiveness of time-sensitive IoT solutions.

92. What is a sensor node in an IoT network?
Answer: A sensor node is a fundamental component in an IoT network that collects data from the environment, such as temperature, motion, or humidity. It typically includes a sensing unit, microcontroller, power source, and communication module. Sensor nodes can process and transmit data to gateways or cloud platforms. They are used in smart homes, agriculture, healthcare, and industrial automation. Due to power and resource constraints, energy efficiency and low data transmission are priorities. The performance of an IoT system heavily depends on the reliability and accuracy of its sensor nodes.

93. What are the security challenges in cloud-based IoT systems?
Answer: Cloud-based IoT systems face numerous security challenges including data breaches, unauthorized access, denial of service attacks, and malware. IoT devices often lack robust security mechanisms, making them vulnerable entry points. When integrated with cloud platforms, the risk extends to data in transit and storage. Challenges include device authentication, secure communication, and ensuring firmware integrity. Best practices include encryption, regular software updates, strong identity management, and endpoint security. Addressing these challenges is vital for user trust, regulatory compliance, and the long-term sustainability of IoT systems.

94. How does blockchain enhance IoT security?
Answer: Blockchain technology enhances IoT security by offering a decentralized and tamper-proof ledger for recording transactions. It ensures data integrity, transparency, and traceability across connected devices. Smart contracts automate actions based on predefined conditions, reducing human intervention and risk. In supply chain IoT, blockchain helps verify product authenticity and track goods. By eliminating central points of failure, blockchain prevents hacking and unauthorized changes. However, implementing blockchain in IoT requires addressing scalability and processing overhead challenges, often through lightweight consensus algorithms and hybrid architectures.

95. What is the role of machine learning in cloud-enabled IoT?
Answer: Machine learning (ML) plays a pivotal role in cloud-enabled IoT by analyzing large volumes of data to identify patterns, make predictions, and automate decisions. Integrated with cloud platforms, ML can process real-time sensor data for anomaly detection, predictive maintenance, or user behavior analysis. For example, in smart energy systems, ML predicts consumption trends to optimize distribution. The cloud provides scalable resources and frameworks like TensorFlow or Azure ML Studio to deploy and manage models. ML enhances IoT by making systems more intelligent, adaptive, and proactive.

96. What is NB-IoT and where is it used?
Answer: NB-IoT (Narrowband Internet of Things) is a low-power wide-area network (LPWAN) technology designed for efficient communication between IoT devices and cellular networks. It supports deep indoor coverage, long battery life, and low data rates, making it ideal for smart meters, environmental sensors, and parking systems. NB-IoT operates within licensed spectrum and integrates with existing LTE infrastructure, ensuring reliable connectivity. Its low cost and wide reach make it suitable for large-scale, low-bandwidth IoT applications in urban and rural settings. Telecom providers worldwide are adopting NB-IoT for various smart city solutions.

97. What are IoT gateways and their function in a network?

Answer: IoT gateways act as intermediaries between IoT devices and cloud platforms. They aggregate data from sensors, perform local processing, and transmit it to the cloud using secure protocols. Gateways also translate communication protocols, manage device authentication, and implement security features like encryption and firewall. In edge computing, gateways execute analytics near the source, reducing latency and bandwidth usage. Their role is crucial in maintaining interoperability, enhancing performance, and ensuring data integrity. IoT gateways are used in industrial automation, healthcare, and transportation to bridge the gap between devices and cloud infrastructure.

98. What is cloud bursting and how is it relevant to IoT?
Answer: Cloud bursting is a hybrid cloud strategy where an application runs in a private cloud or data center and "bursts" into a public cloud when resource demands exceed capacity. In IoT, where workloads can spike due to sensor data surges or event processing, cloud bursting provides the necessary flexibility. It ensures performance continuity without over-provisioning infrastructure. For example, a smart traffic system may burst into the public cloud during peak hours to analyze video streams and traffic data. Cloud bursting helps balance cost, scalability, and performance in dynamic IoT environments.

99. What is the difference between SaaS and PaaS in cloud IoT solutions?
Answer: SaaS (Software as a Service) provides complete applications hosted in the cloud, accessible via web interfaces—ideal for end-users. In IoT, SaaS can be used for monitoring dashboards or analytics tools. PaaS (Platform as a Service), on the other hand, offers a development environment to build, test, and deploy applications. It includes tools, libraries, and infrastructure required for IoT application development. SaaS is ready-to-use, while PaaS gives developers more control and customization options. Choosing between the two depends on business needs, technical expertise, and system complexity.

100. What is telemetry in the context of IoT?
Answer: Telemetry refers to the automatic collection and transmission of data from remote IoT devices to a central system for monitoring and analysis. It involves sensors capturing data like temperature, pressure, or location, which is then sent over communication channels to cloud-based servers. In IoT, telemetry is crucial for real-time tracking, predictive maintenance, and remote diagnostics. It is widely used in smart agriculture, fleet management, and industrial monitoring. Modern telemetry systems leverage protocols like MQTT and REST, cloud analytics, and dashboards to provide actionable insights and improve operational efficiency.

101. What is the role of RESTful APIs in cloud-based IoT systems?
Answer: RESTful APIs are widely used in cloud-based IoT systems for enabling communication between IoT devices and cloud platforms using HTTP protocols. They provide a lightweight, stateless architecture that supports standard operations like GET, POST, PUT, and DELETE, making integration simple and efficient. RESTful APIs allow IoT applications to send and retrieve data to/from cloud servers, interact with databases, or control devices remotely. Due to their scalability, ease of implementation, and compatibility with multiple programming languages, RESTful APIs are ideal for building interoperable and maintainable IoT solutions across various industries like agriculture, health, and smart cities.

102. What is MQTT and how does it work in IoT?
Answer: MQTT (Message Queuing Telemetry Transport) is a lightweight messaging protocol designed for low-bandwidth, high-latency, or unreliable networks—making it ideal for IoT environments. It follows a publish-subscribe model where devices (publishers) send data to a broker, which then forwards it to subscribed clients. This asynchronous communication method ensures efficient data transmission, minimal resource usage, and reliable messaging. MQTT is used extensively in smart homes, industrial automation, and wearable devices. Its features like Quality of Service (QoS), retained messages, and persistent sessions help maintain consistent communication in real-time IoT applications even during network disruptions.

103. What is fog computing and how is it different from cloud computing?
Answer: Fog computing extends cloud computing capabilities to the edge of the network, closer to IoT devices. It reduces latency, minimizes bandwidth usage, and enhances security by processing data locally before sending it to the cloud. Unlike traditional cloud computing that centralizes data processing in remote servers, fog computing uses local nodes like gateways, routers, and switches for intermediate data handling. This architecture is beneficial for time-sensitive applications such as autonomous vehicles or industrial IoT. Fog computing complements the cloud by distributing workloads and enabling faster, context-aware decision-making.

104. What is the function of IoT platforms like AWS IoT or Google Cloud IoT?
Answer: IoT platforms such as AWS IoT and Google Cloud IoT serve as the bridge between connected devices and cloud services. They offer tools for device registration, secure communication, data storage, real-time analytics, machine learning, and remote management. These platforms provide protocols like MQTT, HTTP, and CoAP to support device-to-cloud interactions. For example, AWS IoT Core allows developers to build scalable IoT applications by integrating with services like AWS Lambda and S3. These platforms simplify complex IoT deployments by offering security, scalability, and analytics, making it easier to develop smart solutions across various domains.

105. How do cloud services ensure high availability for IoT systems?
Answer: Cloud services ensure high availability for IoT systems by using geographically distributed data centers, redundancy, load balancing, and failover mechanisms. Service providers like AWS, Azure, and Google Cloud offer Service Level Agreements (SLAs) ensuring uptime of 99.9% or higher. They use auto-scaling features to accommodate variable traffic loads and implement backup systems to avoid data loss. In the event of hardware failure or cyberattacks, these cloud platforms automatically redirect traffic to standby servers. This resilience ensures that IoT devices maintain uninterrupted service, especially in critical sectors like healthcare, smart grid, or logistics.

106. What are the key protocols used in IoT communication?
Answer: IoT communication relies on several protocols, each optimized for specific network conditions and device capabilities. Common protocols include MQTT (lightweight, publish-subscribe), CoAP (for constrained devices), HTTP/HTTPS (web communication), Zigbee and Z-Wave (short-range mesh networks), Bluetooth Low Energy (BLE), and LoRaWAN (long-range, low-power). These protocols help manage data transmission, device control, and interoperability. MQTT and CoAP are preferred for low-power applications, while HTTP is suitable for RESTful APIs. The selection of protocol depends on factors like power consumption, range, bandwidth, and the required security level in the IoT deployment.

107. What is the impact of cloud computing on IoT scalability?
Answer: Cloud computing significantly enhances IoT scalability by offering elastic resources that adjust based on demand. As IoT networks grow, the cloud provides the necessary infrastructure to accommodate millions of connected devices and petabytes of data. Platforms like AWS, Azure, or GCP offer auto-scaling, container orchestration, and serverless computing, which helps manage varying workloads efficiently. Additionally, cloud storage, load balancing, and distributed databases ensure consistent performance during scale-up. This allows businesses to expand their IoT solutions without worrying about infrastructure limitations or increased operational complexity.

108. What is the difference between public, private, and hybrid clouds in IoT?
Answer: Public clouds, like AWS and Azure, offer shared infrastructure and services accessible over the internet. They are cost-effective and scalable, ideal for non-sensitive IoT applications. Private clouds, on the other hand, are dedicated environments for a single organization, offering greater control, security, and customization—suitable for healthcare or finance sectors. Hybrid clouds combine both, enabling data or workloads to move between environments. For instance, sensitive data can be stored in a private cloud, while analytics run in a public cloud. This flexibility helps organizations balance security, cost, and performance in IoT deployments.

109. How does IoT data get stored and managed in the cloud?
Answer: IoT data is typically stored in cloud-based databases and storage services such as Amazon S3, Google Cloud Storage, or Azure Blob Storage. Time-series databases like InfluxDB or AWS Timestream are often used to handle sensor data that changes over time. Cloud platforms also offer data lakes and warehouses for managing large-scale structured and unstructured data. Data pipelines process incoming streams for storage, analytics, or machine learning. Security features such as encryption at rest and in transit, access control, and backup services help ensure data integrity and compliance with regulations.

110. What are the advantages of cloud computing for IoT application development?
Answer: Cloud computing provides developers with tools, infrastructure, and services needed to build, test, deploy, and scale IoT applications quickly. Benefits include on-demand resource provisioning, serverless computing, data analytics, and AI integration. Developers can use cloud SDKs and APIs to streamline connectivity, device management, and real-time monitoring. CI/CD pipelines enable rapid deployment and updates. With services like AWS IoT Core or Google Cloud Functions, development becomes faster, cost-effective, and more agile. These

advantages allow organizations to innovate quickly, reduce time-to-market, and focus on core functionality rather than infrastructure.

111. How does serverless computing support IoT applications?

Answer: Serverless computing, offered by platforms like AWS Lambda or Google Cloud Functions, allows developers to execute backend code without managing servers. In IoT applications, it helps process incoming device data, trigger alerts, store information, and integrate with APIs on demand. Serverless functions automatically scale with traffic, making them cost-efficient for IoT systems that experience variable loads. Developers only pay for the compute time consumed. Serverless architecture accelerates deployment, simplifies maintenance, and ensures responsiveness, making it ideal for real-time IoT scenarios such as home automation, industrial monitoring, or health tracking systems.

112. What is device shadowing in cloud-based IoT platforms?

Answer: Device shadowing refers to maintaining a virtual copy (or "shadow") of an IoT device's state in the cloud. This feature is used in platforms like AWS IoT to keep track of a device's last known status, even when it's offline. Device shadows store metadata like temperature, connectivity status, and operational mode. Applications can read and modify the shadow, which syncs with the device when it reconnects. This enhances reliability and enables offline control, useful in remote environments where devices have intermittent connectivity, such as agriculture fields or offshore equipment.

113. How is data analytics integrated into IoT via the cloud?

Answer: Cloud platforms integrate data analytics by offering tools like AWS Analytics, Google BigQuery, or Azure Synapse to process, visualize, and extract insights from IoT-generated data. IoT devices send streams of data to cloud services where real-time analytics, machine learning, or predictive modeling can be applied. These insights help in anomaly detection, predictive maintenance, or trend forecasting. For instance, a smart thermostat could analyze user patterns to optimize heating schedules. Cloud-based analytics enhance decision-making, operational efficiency, and user experiences in smart homes, healthcare, manufacturing, and beyond.

114. What is real-time processing in IoT cloud applications?

Answer: Real-time processing in IoT cloud applications refers to the ability to ingest, process, and respond to data from devices almost instantly. This is crucial in applications like autonomous vehicles, healthcare monitoring, or industrial automation. Tools like AWS Kinesis, Apache Kafka, and Azure Stream Analytics allow data streams to be analyzed on the fly. Real-time systems help detect anomalies, trigger alerts, or automate responses without delay. Cloud services provide the scalability, speed, and reliability necessary to manage high volumes of streaming data efficiently and securely.

115. What is edge analytics and how is it different from cloud analytics?

Answer: Edge analytics refers to analyzing data directly on edge devices or near the data source rather than sending it to the cloud. This reduces latency, conserves bandwidth, and enhances data privacy. It is suitable for time-sensitive applications like industrial robotics, smart grids, or autonomous systems. In contrast, cloud analytics offers deep processing capabilities, storage, and advanced tools like machine learning and BI dashboards but may introduce delay due to data transmission. A hybrid approach combining edge and cloud analytics is often used to balance speed, complexity, and resource optimization.

116. What is the role of AI and ML in cloud-based IoT systems?

Answer: AI and ML play a transformative role in cloud-based IoT systems by enabling intelligent data analysis, pattern recognition, and predictive decision-making. Machine learning algorithms can identify anomalies, forecast trends, or automate actions based on IoT sensor inputs. For example, in predictive maintenance, AI models can detect equipment failure risks based on vibration or temperature data. Cloud platforms offer integrated services like Google AutoML or AWS SageMaker, making it easier to deploy AI models at scale. This fusion of AI, IoT, and cloud unlocks smarter, autonomous, and adaptive systems.

117. How does Kubernetes support IoT cloud infrastructure?

Answer: Kubernetes is an open-source container orchestration platform that automates deployment, scaling, and management of containerized applications. In IoT cloud infrastructure, Kubernetes supports microservices that manage data ingestion, device communication, analytics, and dashboards. It provides scalability to handle growing numbers of connected devices and ensures high availability via self-healing capabilities. Kubernetes clusters can be deployed across hybrid cloud environments, offering flexibility and resource optimization. Using Kubernetes with IoT enables organizations to develop modular, maintainable, and resilient systems, which is essential for complex deployments like smart cities or industrial automation.

118. What is cloud orchestration in IoT?

Answer: Cloud orchestration in IoT involves automating and coordinating various cloud services and components that support IoT workflows. It manages tasks like provisioning resources, deploying services, load balancing, and scaling across distributed environments. Tools such as Kubernetes, Ansible, and Terraform help orchestrate infrastructure and application layers. In IoT, orchestration ensures that data from devices is routed, stored, analyzed, and visualized seamlessly. It simplifies complex deployments, improves resource efficiency, and ensures smooth integration between services, devices, and applications. This is critical for large-scale IoT projects involving multiple devices and cloud services.

119. What is the concept of Digital Twin in IoT?

Answer: A Digital Twin is a virtual model of a physical IoT device or system that mirrors its real-time data and behavior. It is used for monitoring, simulation, and predictive analysis. Digital Twins collect sensor data via IoT and display insights on dashboards, allowing users to understand performance, predict failures, and test scenarios without physical risk. Cloud platforms like Azure Digital Twins or Siemens MindSphere support building such models. In industries like manufacturing, aviation, and healthcare, Digital Twins optimize operations, reduce downtime, and improve asset management through continuous synchronization between the physical and virtual environments.

120. What are the key differences between fog computing and edge computing in IoT?

Answer: Both fog and edge computing aim to process data closer to the source, reducing latency and dependence on centralized cloud systems. However, edge computing processes data directly on devices or gateways (e.g., sensors, embedded boards), while fog computing uses an intermediate layer—such as routers or local servers—to preprocess data before cloud upload. Edge is device-centric, and fog is network-centric. Fog computing offers more computational resources than edge devices and is suitable for use cases requiring some local analysis with cloud collaboration, like smart traffic systems or energy grids.

Chapter 6: Most Asked Questions Part-B

1. What is containerization and how is it used in IoT cloud deployments?
Answer: Containerization involves packaging an application and its dependencies into a lightweight, portable unit called a container. Tools like Docker are commonly used. In IoT cloud deployments, containerization helps isolate microservices that handle data collection, analysis, or device management. Containers can be deployed across edge, fog, or cloud layers, improving consistency, scalability, and maintainability. Container orchestration platforms like Kubernetes manage the lifecycle of containers, ensuring efficient resource use and high availability. This modular approach allows rapid development and flexible deployment of IoT applications across diverse environments.

2. How does latency affect IoT cloud applications?
Answer: Latency refers to the delay between an IoT device sending data and receiving a response. In IoT cloud applications, high latency can impact real-time systems like autonomous vehicles, medical monitoring, or industrial automation. Factors like network congestion, physical distance, and processing delays in the cloud contribute to latency. To mitigate it, techniques like edge computing, fog computing, and Content Delivery Networks (CDNs) are employed. Reducing latency enhances performance, safety, and user experience. Critical applications often require sub-millisecond latency to function effectively, demanding optimal cloud-architecture planning.

3. What is load balancing and why is it important in IoT cloud systems?
Answer: Load balancing distributes incoming traffic or workloads across multiple servers to ensure no single server is overwhelmed. In IoT cloud systems, where thousands of devices may send data simultaneously, load balancers prevent service disruptions, reduce latency, and enhance reliability. They ensure even resource utilization and support scalability by directing traffic to healthy, responsive instances. Cloud providers like AWS, Azure, and GCP offer integrated load balancing solutions. Effective load balancing is critical for maintaining service quality, especially during traffic spikes in IoT applications like smart cities or connected vehicles.

4. What is CoAP and how does it differ from MQTT?
Answer: CoAP (Constrained Application Protocol) is a web transfer protocol designed for low-power, constrained IoT devices. It is similar to HTTP but optimized for constrained environments and uses UDP instead of TCP. MQTT, on the other hand, is a publish-subscribe protocol designed for lightweight messaging over unreliable networks. While CoAP follows a request-response model, MQTT relies on a broker to route messages between publishers and subscribers. CoAP is ideal for simple, direct client-server interactions, while MQTT is better suited for many-to-many communication in dynamic environments like smart homes or wearables.

5. How does over-the-air (OTA) updates work in IoT cloud systems?
Answer: OTA updates enable remote firmware or software updates of IoT devices via the cloud. The process involves uploading the update package to a cloud platform, which then pushes it to devices based on triggers or schedules. OTA allows manufacturers to fix bugs, enhance features, or patch vulnerabilities without physical access. Cloud services like AWS IoT Device Management provide tools for update rollout, monitoring, and rollback. OTA is vital for security, performance, and lifecycle management of IoT devices, especially those deployed in remote or hard-to-reach areas.

6. What is multitenancy in cloud IoT platforms?
Answer: Multitenancy allows multiple users or organizations (tenants) to share a single cloud infrastructure while keeping their data and operations isolated. In cloud IoT platforms, this enables service providers to offer customized solutions to different clients without setting up separate infrastructures. Each tenant gets personalized dashboards, analytics, and data views. Multitenancy reduces cost, simplifies maintenance, and improves scalability. It is essential for building SaaS-based IoT platforms where multiple clients require independent yet secure access to services like device monitoring, analytics, and control.

7. What is the role of blockchain in IoT and cloud integration?
Answer: Blockchain provides a decentralized, tamper-proof ledger that can enhance security, transparency, and trust in IoT-cloud ecosystems. It is used for secure device authentication, data integrity verification, and traceability in supply chains. Smart contracts automate actions based on predefined rules, reducing manual intervention. Blockchain prevents data manipulation and provides accountability in multi-party environments. Integrating blockchain with

cloud-based IoT ensures secure data sharing among devices, platforms, and users—especially in sectors like finance, logistics, and healthcare where trust and data authenticity are critical.

8. What is ThingSpeak and how is it used in IoT?
Answer: ThingSpeak is an open-source IoT platform for collecting, analyzing, and visualizing sensor data in real time. It supports integration with MATLAB for advanced analytics and processing. Developers use ThingSpeak to create data channels, send readings via HTTP/MQTT, and plot results on customizable dashboards. It is widely used in academic, hobbyist, and prototyping projects for environmental monitoring, smart agriculture, or automation. ThingSpeak's ease of use and free tier make it a popular choice for learning and small-scale deployments, offering essential cloud IoT features with low complexity.

9. What are virtual sensors in IoT?
Answer: Virtual sensors are software-based constructs that estimate physical measurements by combining data from real sensors with mathematical models or machine learning algorithms. They provide insights where physical sensors are impractical, expensive, or unreliable. For example, a virtual sensor may estimate engine torque by analyzing RPM and fuel usage. In IoT cloud systems, virtual sensors reduce hardware costs, improve accuracy, and enhance flexibility. They are commonly used in automotive, manufacturing, and HVAC systems to augment monitoring capabilities and drive smarter decision-making.

10. How do SIM-based IoT devices connect to the cloud?
Answer: SIM-based IoT devices use cellular networks (2G, 3G, 4G, or NB-IoT) to transmit data to cloud platforms. These devices contain M2M or eSIM modules that connect to a mobile operator's network. Once connected, data is sent via secure channels like HTTPS or MQTT to cloud services such as AWS, Azure, or custom IoT servers. These connections are managed by IoT connectivity platforms like Twilio or Hologram. SIM-based connectivity ensures wide coverage and is ideal for mobile or remote applications like asset tracking, fleet management, and environmental sensing.

11. What is MQTT and why is it suitable for IoT?
Answer: MQTT (Message Queuing Telemetry Transport) is a lightweight publish-subscribe messaging protocol ideal for low-bandwidth, high-latency networks—exactly the conditions often found in IoT environments. It works using a broker that routes messages between clients (publishers and subscribers). Its small code footprint, efficient communication, and low power usage make it perfect for constrained devices like sensors, wearables, or embedded systems. MQTT ensures reliable delivery with three QoS levels and supports persistent sessions. It is widely used in smart homes, telemetry, and industrial IoT, where efficient and real-time communication is essential.

12. How does HTTP differ from MQTT in IoT applications?
Answer: HTTP is a request-response protocol typically used for web communications, while MQTT uses a lightweight publish-subscribe model. In IoT, MQTT is preferred because it consumes less bandwidth and works better over unreliable networks. HTTP requires continuous connections and headers, which is inefficient for constrained devices. MQTT, using persistent sessions and brokers, offers better real-time data transmission. HTTP is stateless, while MQTT maintains connection state, making it more suitable for continuous telemetry, such as temperature monitoring or device control in remote IoT applications.

133. What are IoT gateways and their role in cloud architecture?
Answer: IoT gateways act as intermediaries between edge devices and cloud platforms. They aggregate, filter, preprocess, and securely transmit data from multiple devices to the cloud. Gateways can also perform edge analytics, reducing the need for constant cloud communication. This helps in lowering latency, bandwidth consumption, and costs. They often support multiple protocols like ZigBee, MQTT, Bluetooth, and Wi-Fi. In cloud architecture, gateways improve scalability, enhance security by managing authentication and encryption, and provide a local buffer in case of connectivity issues.

14. What is the importance of RESTful APIs in cloud-based IoT?
Answer: RESTful APIs (Representational State Transfer) enable IoT devices and cloud services to communicate using standard HTTP methods like GET, POST, PUT, and DELETE. These APIs allow easy integration, scalability, and flexibility in accessing and controlling devices. In cloud-based IoT, REST APIs facilitate data retrieval, device provisioning, firmware updates, and analytics integration. They're lightweight, platform-independent, and easy to

implement. Most modern IoT platforms like AWS, Azure, and Google Cloud use REST APIs for managing devices and services, enabling developers to create interoperable and scalable solutions efficiently.

15. What is an IoT platform and what are its key components?
Answer: An IoT platform is a multi-layered technology framework that facilitates the management of IoT devices, data, and applications. Key components include device management, data ingestion, analytics, connectivity management, security, cloud integration, and user interfaces. It allows seamless communication between devices and applications. Leading platforms like AWS IoT Core, Microsoft Azure IoT Hub, and Google Cloud IoT offer end-to-end solutions for connecting, monitoring, and analyzing IoT systems. These platforms reduce development time, ensure scalability, and help organizations build robust, secure IoT ecosystems efficiently.

16. What are the benefits of multi-cloud strategy in IoT systems?
Answer: A multi-cloud strategy involves using services from more than one cloud provider. In IoT, this ensures flexibility, avoids vendor lock-in, and allows selecting the best services from different clouds. It enhances reliability—if one provider experiences downtime, another can take over. Cost optimization is possible by choosing the most affordable provider for specific workloads. It also improves compliance and data sovereignty by choosing providers with data centers in specific regions. For example, using AWS for device management and Google Cloud for analytics offers performance and cost advantages.

17. What is a sensor network and how does it relate to IoT?
Answer: A sensor network is a group of interconnected sensors that collect and transmit data about physical conditions like temperature, pressure, motion, or humidity. These networks are core components of IoT, enabling devices to monitor and interact with their environments. Data from sensor networks is transmitted to a central system (cloud or edge gateway) for processing and analysis. Applications include smart agriculture (soil moisture sensors), industrial automation (vibration sensors), and environmental monitoring (air quality sensors). Cloud integration allows real-time monitoring, alerting, and predictive analytics based on sensor data.

18. How does GPS work in IoT devices?
Answer: GPS (Global Positioning System) is used in IoT for tracking and location-based services. Devices with GPS modules receive signals from a constellation of satellites to determine their exact location. In IoT, GPS is used in applications like vehicle tracking, asset management, and smart logistics. The location data is often transmitted to cloud platforms for visualization, geofencing, and route optimization. Low-power GPS modules and assisted GPS (A-GPS) help optimize performance and battery usage in IoT deployments where energy conservation is crucial.

19. What is a microcontroller and how is it used in IoT?
Answer: A microcontroller (MCU) is a compact integrated circuit containing a processor, memory, and input/output peripherals on a single chip. In IoT, microcontrollers serve as the brains of devices—reading sensor data, processing information, and sending it to the cloud. Popular MCUs like Arduino, ESP8266, or STM32 are widely used in smart devices, wearables, and embedded systems. They are chosen for low power consumption, real-time processing, and affordability. Programming MCUs with embedded software allows them to interact autonomously or respond to cloud-based commands.

20. What is Azure IoT Hub and how does it work?
Answer: Azure IoT Hub is Microsoft's cloud platform for managing and scaling IoT solutions. It provides secure device-to-cloud and cloud-to-device communication, device provisioning, and monitoring. Devices send telemetry data to IoT Hub via protocols like MQTT or HTTPS. This data can then be routed to Azure services like Stream Analytics or Machine Learning for further processing. IoT Hub also supports bi-directional communication for commands, updates, or device reboots. Built-in security features include per-device authentication and message encryption, making Azure IoT Hub a robust, scalable solution for enterprise IoT deployments.

21. What is AWS IoT Core and what are its features?
Answer: AWS IoT Core is Amazon's managed cloud platform that lets connected devices interact securely with cloud applications and other devices. Features include device registry, MQTT/HTTP communication, message routing, authentication, and integration with other AWS services like Lambda, S3, or DynamoDB. AWS IoT Core supports rules engines, enabling automatic actions based on incoming data. It offers high scalability and supports billions of

devices. Security is maintained via mutual TLS authentication and fine-grained access control. It's widely used in industrial automation, smart homes, and connected vehicles.

22. What is Zigbee and its role in IoT?
Answer: Zigbee is a low-power, short-range wireless communication protocol designed for IoT and home automation applications. It supports mesh networking, where devices relay data to each other, increasing range and reliability. Zigbee is commonly used in smart lighting, home security systems, and environmental sensors. It consumes less power than Wi-Fi, making it ideal for battery-operated devices. Zigbee's standardization and interoperability across vendors make it a popular choice in consumer and industrial IoT deployments. Devices communicate using a central coordinator, which often connects to a cloud gateway.

23. How do IoT devices authenticate with cloud platforms?
Answer: IoT devices authenticate with cloud platforms using secure credentials like X.509 certificates, symmetric keys, or OAuth tokens. This ensures that only authorized devices can connect and exchange data. Cloud platforms like AWS IoT and Azure IoT Hub support per-device authentication and encryption via TLS (Transport Layer Security). Some platforms also allow multi-factor authentication and hardware security modules (HSMs) for added protection. Authentication is critical for maintaining data integrity, device trust, and preventing unauthorized access in large-scale IoT ecosystems.

24. What is a device registry in IoT platforms?
Answer: A device registry is a central component of an IoT platform that stores metadata about connected devices, including ID, type, status, credentials, and configuration settings. It helps platforms manage and monitor devices efficiently. When a device connects to the cloud, the registry verifies its identity and updates its status. It supports tasks like firmware updates, diagnostics, and command issuance. Examples include AWS IoT Device Registry and Azure IoT Hub Device Identity Registry. The registry plays a key role in managing device lifecycles securely and efficiently.

25. What are the security challenges in cloud-based IoT?
Answer: Cloud-based IoT systems face several security challenges:
Data Breaches – Sensitive data can be intercepted if not encrypted.
Unauthorized Access – Weak authentication can allow attackers to control devices.
Insecure APIs – Poorly secured interfaces can be exploited.
Firmware Vulnerabilities – Outdated firmware is a common attack vector.
Denial of Service (DoS) – Large volumes of traffic can overload systems.
To address these, organizations must implement encryption, strong authentication, regular updates, access controls, and real-time threat detection.

26. What is the significance of OTA firmware updates?
Answer: OTA (Over-the-Air) firmware updates allow IoT devices to be remotely updated with new software or patches without requiring physical access. This is essential for maintaining security, fixing bugs, and introducing new features. OTA reduces maintenance costs and downtime, especially in large or geographically distributed device fleets. Cloud platforms support secure OTA via version control, rollout policies, and fallback mechanisms. For example, smart home devices can receive periodic updates to improve compatibility or security, enhancing device longevity and performance.

27. How is bandwidth optimization achieved in IoT systems?
Answer: Bandwidth optimization in IoT involves reducing the amount of data transmitted without compromising functionality. Techniques include:
Edge computing: Processing data locally to send only necessary information.
Data compression: Using algorithms to reduce payload size.
Event-driven architecture: Sending data only upon specific triggers.
Efficient protocols: MQTT, CoAP consume less bandwidth than HTTP.
Optimization is critical in remote IoT deployments where connectivity is limited or expensive, such as agriculture or offshore monitoring systems.

28. What is a cloud function and how is it used in IoT?

Answer: A cloud function is a lightweight, serverless compute service that runs in response to events. In IoT, cloud functions process incoming data, trigger alerts, or update device status. For example, when a temperature sensor exceeds a threshold, a function can send an SMS alert or shut down a machine. Functions scale automatically and reduce costs by executing only when triggered. Popular platforms include AWS Lambda, Google Cloud Functions, and Azure Functions. Cloud functions streamline development and improve responsiveness in IoT systems.

29. What is Industrial IoT (IIoT)?
Answer: Industrial IoT refers to the use of IoT technologies in manufacturing and industrial sectors to enhance efficiency, safety, and automation. It involves connecting sensors, machines, and control systems to cloud platforms for real-time monitoring and predictive maintenance. IIoT enables smart factories, energy optimization, and improved asset management. Common applications include SCADA integration, predictive analytics, and remote diagnostics. IIoT relies heavily on cloud computing, edge analytics, and AI to optimize operations, reduce downtime, and improve decision-making.

30. What is a smart contract and how is it applied in IoT?
Answer: A smart contract is a self-executing digital agreement stored on a blockchain. In IoT, it can automate actions based on predefined rules. For example, a smart meter could trigger a payment once energy usage exceeds a limit. Smart contracts enhance trust, remove intermediaries, and ensure transparency in multi-party IoT applications like supply chains or asset tracking. By combining IoT data and blockchain logic, smart contracts provide tamper-proof, efficient automation and enforce rules without manual oversight.

31. What is the concept of elastic computing in cloud computing?
Answer: Elastic computing refers to the ability of cloud services to dynamically allocate and deallocate computing resources as needed. It ensures that applications can scale up during peak usage times and scale down during periods of low demand, optimizing resource usage and minimizing costs. This flexibility is crucial for businesses that experience fluctuating workloads, such as e-commerce sites during sales. Elastic computing is typically achieved through automation, orchestration tools, and virtualization. Services like AWS EC2 Auto Scaling, Azure Virtual Machine Scale Sets, and Kubernetes enable elastic scaling. The key benefit is efficiency—resources are used only when required, reducing waste and ensuring high availability.

32. How does IoT contribute to smart agriculture?
Answer: IoT enhances smart agriculture by introducing automation, monitoring, and data-driven decision-making. Sensors placed in the field monitor soil moisture, temperature, humidity, and crop health in real-time. This data is sent to cloud platforms for analysis, enabling farmers to optimize irrigation, fertilization, and pest control. IoT devices can also track livestock movement and monitor storage conditions for crops. Drones and GPS technologies provide aerial views and map large areas quickly. This results in increased productivity, reduced waste, and sustainable farming practices. Smart agriculture powered by IoT improves efficiency, conserves resources, and helps meet the growing global food demand.

33. What is a Cloud Orchestrator and how does it work?
Answer: A cloud orchestrator is a management tool that automates and coordinates various cloud services, ensuring that resources work together efficiently. It handles provisioning, deployment, configuration, and scaling of cloud infrastructure. Orchestration tools like Kubernetes, Terraform, and AWS CloudFormation automate repetitive tasks, reduce human error, and enforce consistency across environments. Cloud orchestrators also manage dependencies, monitor service health, and apply policy-based governance. In multi-cloud or hybrid cloud setups, orchestrators ensure interoperability and streamlined operations. They are essential for DevOps and CI/CD workflows, enabling rapid and reliable application development and deployment.

34. What are the benefits of using edge computing in IoT systems?
Answer: Edge computing processes data closer to the source—IoT devices—rather than relying solely on cloud data centers. This reduces latency, improves response time, and conserves bandwidth by processing critical data locally. It's particularly beneficial for time-sensitive applications like autonomous vehicles, smart manufacturing, and healthcare monitoring. Edge computing also enhances data privacy, as sensitive data need not be transmitted to the cloud. In cases of network failure, edge devices can still function independently. By distributing workloads, edge computing improves system resilience and reduces dependence on internet connectivity, making IoT applications more robust and efficient.

35. What is Platform as a Service (PaaS) in cloud computing?
Answer: Platform as a Service (PaaS) is a cloud delivery model that provides a platform and environment for developers to build, deploy, and manage applications. It offers a complete development framework with tools for coding, testing, and deployment, along with underlying infrastructure like servers, storage, and networking. PaaS eliminates the need for managing hardware and software layers, allowing developers to focus on application logic. Examples include Google App Engine and Microsoft Azure App Services. PaaS supports faster development cycles, scalability, and integration with databases and analytics tools, making it ideal for agile and DevOps-based development.

36. How does fog computing differ from edge computing in IoT?
Answer: While both fog and edge computing reduce reliance on centralized cloud data centers, they differ in scope and architecture. Edge computing processes data directly on IoT devices or nearby gateways. In contrast, fog computing introduces an intermediate layer between the edge and cloud, providing additional processing, storage, and analytics capabilities. Fog nodes can coordinate multiple edge devices, support larger-scale analytics, and enforce policies across devices. Fog computing is often used in industrial IoT, smart cities, and transportation networks, where local processing needs to be distributed across regions. Together, fog and edge computing enhance the efficiency, scalability, and reliability of IoT systems.

37. What are the common protocols used in IoT communication?
Answer: IoT systems use a variety of protocols to communicate effectively between devices and cloud services. Common application layer protocols include MQTT (lightweight and ideal for low-power devices), CoAP (optimized for constrained environments), and HTTP/HTTPS (used for web-based communication). Network layer protocols include IPv6 and 6LoWPAN. For device-to-device communication, Zigbee, Bluetooth Low Energy (BLE), and Z-Wave are widely used. LoRaWAN and NB-IoT are used for long-range, low-power wide-area networks. These protocols are selected based on energy consumption, range, bandwidth, and real-time requirements. Their standardization ensures interoperability and reliability in diverse IoT environments.

38. What is auto-scaling in cloud computing and why is it important?
Answer: Auto-scaling is the process by which cloud platforms automatically adjust the number of computing resources based on current demand. If the workload increases, the system scales out (adds more resources); if it decreases, it scales in (removes resources). This ensures optimal performance, cost-efficiency, and availability. Auto-scaling is vital for applications with variable traffic, such as e-commerce, streaming services, or seasonal apps. It eliminates manual intervention, reduces the risk of service downtime, and ensures users experience consistent performance. AWS Auto Scaling, Azure VM Scale Sets, and Kubernetes Horizontal Pod Autoscaler are commonly used tools for implementing auto-scaling.

39. How does cloud computing enhance the scalability of IoT applications?
Answer: Cloud computing provides a flexible, on-demand infrastructure that supports the growing scale of IoT ecosystems. As the number of connected devices increases, cloud services allow for rapid expansion of storage, processing power, and networking capabilities. Cloud platforms support load balancing, containerization, and distributed databases that help IoT applications scale seamlessly. With services like AWS IoT Core or Azure IoT Hub, developers can connect and manage millions of devices. Additionally, cloud computing offers analytics, AI integration, and monitoring tools that enable real-time insights and automation, making large-scale IoT deployments efficient, reliable, and cost-effective.

40. What is the role of API gateways in cloud-based IoT architectures?
Answer: API gateways serve as the entry point for client requests in cloud-based IoT architectures. They manage and route API calls from IoT devices to backend services. Their key functions include request validation, rate limiting, authentication, logging, and protocol translation. API gateways simplify the integration of diverse IoT devices and services, ensuring security and scalability. By centralizing access control and traffic management, they protect backend systems from overload or malicious attacks. Popular API gateways like AWS API Gateway or Azure API Management help developers build, deploy, and monitor secure APIs, enabling robust communication between IoT networks and cloud platforms.

41. How is serverless computing used in IoT applications?

Answer: Serverless computing allows developers to build and deploy applications without managing servers. In IoT, serverless architectures are used to process events triggered by sensors or devices, such as motion detection or temperature thresholds. Cloud providers like AWS Lambda or Azure Functions run small pieces of code (functions) in response to these events, scaling automatically and charging only for execution time. This model is highly cost-effective and ideal for lightweight, event-driven IoT applications. It reduces operational overhead, accelerates development, and enables integration with databases, analytics, and other cloud services, making it a powerful tool in real-time IoT ecosystems.

42. What are the security risks associated with cloud-based IoT systems?
Answer: Cloud-based IoT systems face several security challenges including data breaches, unauthorized access, device hijacking, and denial-of-service attacks. Since IoT devices often have limited computing power, they may lack robust security features. When connected to the cloud, vulnerabilities can be exploited to intercept or manipulate data. Risks also include poor authentication, unsecured APIs, and unpatched firmware. Securing such systems requires encryption, strong identity management, intrusion detection systems, and regular updates. Compliance with standards like ISO/IEC 27001 and implementing network segmentation also help mitigate risks. Continuous monitoring is crucial for detecting anomalies and protecting user privacy and operational integrity.

43. How does virtualization support cloud computing?
Answer: Virtualization enables multiple virtual machines (VMs) to run on a single physical server, each with its own operating system and resources. It allows cloud providers to optimize hardware utilization, isolate workloads, and deploy scalable services. Through hypervisors like VMware, KVM, or Hyper-V, virtualization abstracts hardware and provides flexible, dynamic environments. This underpins cloud models like IaaS, where users can provision and manage virtual servers. Virtualization improves disaster recovery, enhances resource allocation, and simplifies system maintenance. It's foundational to the cloud's ability to offer elastic, pay-per-use services, making it a key enabler of modern cloud infrastructure.

44. What is the role of MQTT protocol in IoT?
Answer: MQTT (Message Queuing Telemetry Transport) is a lightweight, publish-subscribe messaging protocol widely used in IoT for its efficiency in constrained environments. Designed to minimize bandwidth and power usage, MQTT operates over TCP/IP and is ideal for devices with limited resources or unreliable networks. In this protocol, clients publish messages to topics, and subscribers receive messages based on their topic subscriptions. A central broker manages this communication. MQTT supports Quality of Service (QoS) levels, message retention, and last will messages, making it reliable for remote sensing, telemetry, and real-time monitoring. It is a popular choice for smart homes and industrial IoT.

45. How does big data analytics support IoT applications?
Answer: Big data analytics plays a critical role in extracting meaningful insights from the massive volumes of data generated by IoT devices. Using tools like Apache Hadoop, Spark, or cloud-based analytics platforms, organizations can process structured and unstructured IoT data for trend analysis, anomaly detection, and predictive maintenance. For example, in manufacturing, sensor data can reveal equipment performance patterns and predict failures. In smart cities, analytics help optimize traffic flow and energy usage. The integration of machine learning further enhances decision-making. Big data analytics transforms raw IoT data into actionable intelligence, driving innovation and efficiency across industries.

46. What is cloud-native architecture in IoT systems?
Answer: Cloud-native architecture involves designing applications specifically for cloud environments using microservices, containers, APIs, and continuous delivery. In IoT, this architecture allows for scalable, resilient, and easily updatable systems. Each microservice handles a specific function, such as device registration, data ingestion, or analytics. Containers (like Docker) package and isolate these services, making them portable across cloud platforms. Orchestration tools like Kubernetes manage container deployment and scaling. Cloud-native IoT systems benefit from faster development, easier scaling, and fault tolerance. This approach is ideal for large-scale IoT deployments where agility, uptime, and rapid iteration are critical.

47. How do IoT and AI work together in cloud environments?
Answer: IoT and AI complement each other when integrated in cloud environments. IoT devices collect real-time data, which is transmitted to the cloud for processing. AI algorithms analyze this data to detect patterns, predict

outcomes, and make decisions. For instance, in smart manufacturing, AI can identify machine anomalies from IoT sensor data to prevent breakdowns. In smart homes, AI learns user behavior to optimize energy usage. Cloud platforms provide the computational power and storage needed for AI model training and deployment. This synergy enhances automation, personalization, and operational efficiency across multiple sectors.

48. What is latency and why is it important in IoT?
Answer: Latency refers to the delay between the initiation of a command or data transmission and the response or action taken. In IoT, low latency is critical for time-sensitive applications like autonomous vehicles, healthcare monitoring, or industrial automation. High latency can result in slow responses, safety risks, or system inefficiencies. Factors affecting latency include network congestion, physical distance to cloud servers, and processing delays. Edge computing and local data processing are used to minimize latency by bringing computation closer to the data source. Monitoring and optimizing latency ensures that IoT systems perform reliably and meet real-time requirements.

49. What are the benefits of using containers in IoT cloud platforms?
Answer: Containers, such as those created with Docker, package an application and its dependencies into a portable unit that can run consistently across environments. In IoT cloud platforms, containers offer scalability, faster deployment, and efficient resource utilization. They simplify development and testing by ensuring uniform environments. Containers are lightweight compared to virtual machines, which is advantageous for resource-constrained IoT applications. With orchestration tools like Kubernetes, containers can be managed dynamically, enabling rapid scaling based on device data loads. Containers support modular architectures and facilitate continuous integration and delivery, making them ideal for agile IoT cloud development.

50. How does Blockchain enhance IoT security?
Answer: Blockchain enhances IoT security by providing a decentralized, tamper-proof ledger for data transactions. Each transaction is recorded in blocks and linked cryptographically, making unauthorized alterations virtually impossible. In IoT, blockchain can secure device identity, authenticate data sources, and prevent malicious data injection. Smart contracts can automate interactions between devices without centralized control. This decentralized trust model is particularly useful in supply chain tracking, autonomous vehicles, and healthcare IoT, where data integrity and trust are crucial. Blockchain also reduces reliance on centralized databases, which can be single points of failure or attack in traditional IoT architectures.

51. What is Identity and Access Management (IAM) in cloud computing?
Answer: Identity and Access Management (IAM) is a framework of policies and technologies ensuring that the right individuals or devices have the appropriate access to cloud resources. It involves authentication (verifying identity) and authorization (granting permissions). IAM services like AWS IAM or Azure Active Directory allow administrators to create users, define roles, and apply policies. IAM is essential for securing cloud applications, especially in IoT where thousands of devices may connect to the network. Proper IAM practices, including multi-factor authentication and least-privilege access, prevent unauthorized access, reduce data breaches, and enforce compliance.

52. What is hybrid cloud and how is it used in IoT?
Answer: A hybrid cloud combines private and public cloud infrastructures, allowing data and applications to be shared between them. In IoT, hybrid cloud enables organizations to process sensitive data locally in a private cloud for security and compliance while leveraging the public cloud for scalable storage and analytics. For example, a hospital may store patient data on-premises but analyze usage trends on the public cloud. This approach offers flexibility, cost efficiency, and improved data governance. Hybrid cloud also enhances business continuity and provides the ability to gradually migrate workloads to the cloud.

53. What is the function of a gateway in IoT networks?
Answer: An IoT gateway acts as a bridge between IoT devices and cloud platforms. It aggregates data from devices, performs local processing or filtering, and transmits relevant information to the cloud. Gateways often support protocol translation (e.g., Zigbee to MQTT), device management, and security functions like encryption and authentication. They reduce bandwidth usage by processing data locally and improve response time by enabling edge analytics. In industrial settings, gateways connect legacy equipment to modern IoT systems. Their role is crucial in ensuring interoperability, security, and reliable communication in distributed IoT architectures.

54. What is data ingestion in IoT cloud platforms?
Answer: Data ingestion refers to the process of collecting, importing, and processing real-time or batch data from IoT devices into cloud platforms. This data is often streamed continuously and includes readings from sensors, logs, or status updates. IoT cloud platforms like AWS IoT, Azure IoT Hub, and Google Cloud IoT Core use data ingestion pipelines to handle high volumes efficiently. These pipelines may include message brokers, stream processors, and data storage services. Effective data ingestion ensures low latency, supports real-time analytics, and enables integration with machine learning and business intelligence tools.

55. What is network slicing and how does it relate to IoT and cloud?
Answer: Network slicing is a 5G technology that creates multiple virtual networks (slices) on a shared physical infrastructure, each optimized for different use cases. In IoT and cloud, network slicing allows tailored services for applications with diverse requirements—such as high bandwidth for video surveillance or ultra-low latency for industrial automation. Each slice can be managed independently with its own performance, security, and reliability parameters. This ensures efficient resource usage and quality of service. Network slicing enhances the performance and flexibility of IoT deployments, especially in smart cities and mission-critical applications.

56. What are the major IoT communication protocols used in healthcare devices?
Answer: In healthcare IoT devices, major communication protocols include Bluetooth Low Energy (BLE), Zigbee, Wi-Fi, MQTT (Message Queuing Telemetry Transport), and CoAP (Constrained Application Protocol). BLE and Zigbee are suitable for low-power, short-range communication, ideal for wearables and medical monitoring devices. MQTT, due to its lightweight nature, is highly preferred in remote monitoring applications because it minimizes bandwidth usage and enables real-time data transmission. CoAP, optimized for constrained environments, works well in devices with limited resources. These protocols ensure seamless and secure data transmission, which is critical in patient monitoring systems, emergency response setups, and electronic health records integration.

57. How does fog computing improve IoT efficiency?
Answer: Fog computing enhances IoT efficiency by processing data closer to the source—at the network edge—rather than relying solely on centralized cloud servers. This reduces latency, conserves bandwidth, and improves response times, which is critical for time-sensitive applications like autonomous vehicles or industrial automation. By analyzing data locally, fog nodes can filter irrelevant information, sending only meaningful data to the cloud, thus optimizing storage and processing power. It also supports better security and compliance, as sensitive data can be processed locally. Overall, fog computing complements cloud computing by delivering real-time intelligence and responsiveness to IoT ecosystems.

58. What is the role of virtualization in cloud computing?
Answer: Virtualization is the foundational technology behind cloud computing, enabling multiple virtual machines (VMs) to run on a single physical server. It abstracts hardware resources—CPU, storage, and memory—so they can be shared among multiple users or applications efficiently. This leads to improved resource utilization, scalability, and isolation between different environments. Virtualization facilitates infrastructure as a service (IaaS), where users can provision VMs on-demand. It also supports disaster recovery and load balancing. By decoupling software from hardware, virtualization allows cloud providers to offer flexible, elastic, and cost-effective services, making it central to modern cloud architectures.

59. What are wearable IoT devices and their applications?
Answer: Wearable IoT devices are smart electronic gadgets worn on the body that connect to the internet and collect data related to health, fitness, and environment. Examples include fitness trackers, smartwatches, wearable ECG monitors, and smart glasses. These devices monitor parameters like heart rate, steps taken, calories burned, sleep quality, and even blood oxygen levels. In healthcare, they assist in chronic disease management and remote patient monitoring. In sports, they provide real-time performance analytics. Some wearables also support augmented reality for industrial or educational use. Their ability to collect real-time data makes them invaluable in both personal and professional applications.

60. What is container orchestration in cloud environments?
Answer: Container orchestration refers to the automated management of containerized applications across clusters of machines. It handles tasks like deployment, scaling, load balancing, and monitoring. Kubernetes is the most widely used orchestration platform, enabling efficient container scheduling and fault tolerance. Orchestration simplifies

managing microservices architectures, where applications are broken into smaller, independent components. It ensures that containers run smoothly, resources are allocated optimally, and applications remain available despite failures. In a cloud environment, orchestration is crucial for continuous delivery, scaling applications dynamically, and ensuring consistency across different environments—development, testing, and production.

61. What is the difference between public and private cloud in terms of control and security?
Answer: Public cloud is a multi-tenant environment where services and infrastructure are shared among multiple users. While cost-effective and scalable, control over data and infrastructure is limited. In contrast, private cloud is dedicated to a single organization, providing enhanced control, customization, and security. Private clouds are ideal for businesses with strict compliance requirements, sensitive data, or proprietary workloads. They allow tailored access control, encryption, and policy enforcement. Public clouds rely on the provider's security protocols, while private clouds can be built on-premise or hosted externally with full organizational governance. The choice depends on the organization's needs for security, control, and cost.

62. What are edge analytics in IoT?
Answer: Edge analytics refers to the real-time data processing and analysis that occurs at the edge of a network, near the data source—such as sensors or IoT devices—rather than in a centralized cloud or data center. It enables faster decision-making, reduces bandwidth usage, and improves system responsiveness. This is particularly useful in applications like predictive maintenance, autonomous driving, and industrial automation. By analyzing data locally, only relevant information is transmitted to the cloud, reducing latency and ensuring timely actions. Edge analytics enhances scalability, reliability, and real-time capabilities, making it essential in modern IoT deployments with time-sensitive operations.

63. What is OpenStack and how does it support cloud computing?
Answer: OpenStack is an open-source cloud computing platform that provides infrastructure as a service (IaaS) by managing large pools of compute, storage, and networking resources through a dashboard or APIs. It supports private and public cloud deployments and is widely adopted due to its flexibility and modular architecture. OpenStack allows organizations to build and manage their own cloud environments, giving them full control over data and infrastructure. Components like Nova (compute), Swift (storage), and Neutron (networking) provide scalable and customizable services. OpenStack enables cost-effective, vendor-neutral cloud solutions, making it suitable for enterprises, telecoms, and research institutions.

64. What are the common IoT challenges in agriculture?
Answer: Common IoT challenges in agriculture include poor network connectivity in rural areas, limited power sources for field devices, high deployment costs, and data integration issues. Ensuring sensor durability in harsh weather and securing sensitive farm data from cyber threats are also significant concerns. Additionally, farmers may face difficulties in interpreting large volumes of data generated by IoT systems. Lack of standardization in devices and protocols can hinder interoperability. Addressing these challenges requires robust infrastructure, affordable solutions, farmer training, and government or private sector support to promote smart farming and precision agriculture at scale.

65. What is cloud bursting in hybrid cloud computing?
Answer: Cloud bursting is a hybrid cloud strategy where an application primarily runs in a private cloud or on-premises infrastructure but can "burst" into a public cloud when additional resources are needed. This approach helps manage sudden spikes in workload without overprovisioning internal resources. It ensures scalability, cost-efficiency, and flexibility by leveraging the elasticity of public clouds only when required. Cloud bursting is ideal for unpredictable workloads like seasonal web traffic or big data processing. However, it requires careful integration, network configuration, and security measures to ensure seamless performance and data consistency across environments.

66. How does NB-IoT support large-scale IoT deployments?
Answer: Narrowband IoT (NB-IoT) is a low-power wide-area network (LPWAN) technology developed for efficient communication between IoT devices and cellular networks. It supports large-scale deployments by offering extended coverage, low power consumption, and cost-effective module pricing. NB-IoT enables long battery life (up to 10 years), which is ideal for applications like smart metering, environmental monitoring, and asset tracking. Its deep indoor penetration makes it suitable for underground or remote installations. NB-IoT uses licensed spectrum, ensuring

reliability and security. It supports massive machine-type communication (mMTC), which is a key requirement for scaling IoT ecosystems in smart cities and industries.

67. What is cloud-native application development?

Answer: Cloud-native application development refers to designing, building, and deploying applications specifically for cloud environments using modern technologies like containers, microservices, DevOps, and continuous integration/continuous delivery (CI/CD). These applications are scalable, resilient, and easily manageable across distributed infrastructure. Cloud-native apps take full advantage of cloud features like elasticity, automated scaling, and resource optimization. They are platform-agnostic and can be deployed in hybrid or multi-cloud setups. By embracing modular design, developers can update components independently, enabling rapid innovation and reduced downtime. Cloud-native development is key to digital transformation and agile business practices.

68. What is MQTT and why is it preferred in IoT?

Answer: MQTT (Message Queuing Telemetry Transport) is a lightweight, publish-subscribe messaging protocol designed for low-bandwidth, high-latency, or unreliable networks, making it ideal for IoT applications. It operates over TCP/IP and requires minimal resources, which suits constrained devices like sensors and microcontrollers. MQTT's simplicity, efficiency, and support for Quality of Service (QoS) levels ensure reliable message delivery. It enables decoupling between devices, reducing interdependencies and allowing for scalable IoT architectures. Due to its small code footprint and robust communication model, MQTT is widely adopted in smart home systems, industrial monitoring, and mobile applications.

69. What is the impact of 5G on cloud and IoT integration?

Answer: The rollout of 5G networks significantly enhances cloud and IoT integration by offering ultra-low latency, higher bandwidth, and massive connectivity. It supports real-time communication for critical applications like autonomous vehicles, remote surgeries, and industrial automation. 5G enables faster data transmission from IoT devices to cloud platforms, making edge computing more effective. Its support for massive machine-type communication (mMTC) facilitates the deployment of millions of connected devices per square kilometer. Additionally, network slicing in 5G allows dedicated virtual networks for different use cases, ensuring QoS and security. Overall, 5G accelerates the adoption and efficiency of cloud-powered IoT ecosystems.

70. How does DevOps benefit cloud-based IoT projects?

Answer: DevOps enhances cloud-based IoT projects by promoting collaboration, continuous integration, and automated deployment. It bridges the gap between development and operations, resulting in faster delivery, improved quality, and reduced downtime. In IoT, where software updates for firmware and device configurations are frequent, DevOps ensures efficient rollout and rollback mechanisms. Automation tools streamline testing and deployment pipelines, while monitoring tools provide real-time visibility into system performance. DevOps practices like Infrastructure as Code (IaC) support consistent and scalable cloud environments. By adopting DevOps, organizations can innovate rapidly and maintain stability across diverse IoT ecosystems.

71. What is IoT security and why is it important?

Answer: IoT security refers to the strategies, technologies, and practices used to protect connected devices and networks in the Internet of Things ecosystem. As IoT devices often collect and transmit sensitive data—such as personal health metrics or industrial control commands—they become prime targets for cyberattacks. Ensuring robust security is crucial to prevent data breaches, device hijacking, and privacy violations. Security measures may include strong authentication, encrypted communication, regular firmware updates, and network segmentation. Given the vast number and diversity of IoT devices, security must be integrated at every level, from hardware and software to cloud infrastructure and user access.

72. What is the role of RESTful APIs in IoT and cloud systems?

Answer: RESTful APIs (Representational State Transfer Application Programming Interfaces) play a critical role in enabling communication between IoT devices and cloud platforms. They allow lightweight, scalable, and stateless interactions using standard HTTP methods such as GET, POST, PUT, and DELETE. RESTful APIs simplify the integration of various devices, applications, and services by providing a uniform interface for data exchange. In IoT, RESTful APIs help sensors and actuators send data to cloud servers or retrieve instructions. They also enable remote control and monitoring, making systems interoperable and easier to manage. REST's simplicity and wide adoption make it ideal for web-connected IoT environments.

73. How does cloud computing facilitate remote IoT device management?

Answer: Cloud computing provides a centralized platform for monitoring, updating, and controlling IoT devices deployed across different geographical locations. Through cloud dashboards and management tools, administrators can access real-time device status, push firmware updates, configure settings, and receive alerts. This eliminates the need for physical access to each device, significantly reducing maintenance costs and effort. Cloud services also support automation and scalability, allowing management of thousands or millions of devices simultaneously. Integration with analytics and AI further enables predictive maintenance and optimization. Thus, cloud computing enhances the efficiency, flexibility, and responsiveness of IoT device management at scale.

74. What is the impact of AI on IoT data analytics?

Answer: Artificial Intelligence (AI) significantly enhances IoT data analytics by enabling intelligent decision-making based on the vast amount of real-time data generated by connected devices. AI algorithms can detect patterns, predict future events, and automate responses, adding a layer of cognitive capability to raw data. For example, in smart homes, AI can learn user behavior to optimize energy use. In healthcare, AI processes sensor data to detect anomalies in patient vitals. In industrial settings, predictive maintenance uses AI to foresee equipment failures before they happen. Overall, AI transforms IoT data into actionable insights, improving efficiency, accuracy, and personalization.

75. What is LoRaWAN and how is it useful in IoT applications?

Answer: LoRaWAN (Long Range Wide Area Network) is a low-power, long-range communication protocol designed for IoT applications that require secure, energy-efficient data transmission over vast distances. It is ideal for use cases such as smart agriculture, asset tracking, environmental monitoring, and smart cities. LoRaWAN operates in the unlicensed spectrum and supports bidirectional communication between devices and gateways, which then connect to cloud platforms. The protocol offers features like end-to-end encryption, adaptive data rates, and scalability to millions of devices. Its ability to function in remote, infrastructure-poor areas with minimal power makes it a leading choice for IoT networks.

76. What is multi-cloud strategy and its relevance to IoT?

Answer: A multi-cloud strategy involves using services from more than one cloud provider to meet different business or technical requirements. For IoT systems, a multi-cloud approach can improve availability, reduce vendor lock-in, and allow data and workloads to be distributed for performance optimization. It enables organizations to leverage specialized services from different providers—such as AWS IoT Core, Azure IoT Hub, or Google Cloud IoT—for different aspects of their IoT infrastructure. Moreover, multi-cloud enhances disaster recovery and resilience by avoiding single points of failure. Effective management tools are required to ensure data consistency, security, and compliance across all platforms involved.

77. How do cloud platforms handle IoT big data challenges?

Answer: Cloud platforms address the big data challenges of IoT by offering scalable storage, distributed computing, and advanced analytics tools. Services such as AWS Kinesis, Google BigQuery, and Azure Stream Analytics are designed to handle large volumes of real-time data generated by millions of devices. Cloud platforms provide the elasticity to scale infrastructure as needed, ensuring uninterrupted data flow and processing. They also support machine learning integration, which helps derive insights from complex datasets. Data lakes, NoSQL databases, and time-series databases are commonly used to store structured and unstructured IoT data efficiently. This enables timely decision-making and long-term trend analysis.

78. What is the significance of Identity and Access Management (IAM) in cloud-based IoT?

Answer: Identity and Access Management (IAM) plays a crucial role in cloud-based IoT by ensuring that only authorized users and devices can access resources. IAM frameworks enable the definition of policies, roles, and permissions that control who can access specific data, services, or devices. In an IoT environment with numerous endpoints, IAM helps maintain security by preventing unauthorized access and reducing the risk of data breaches. It also supports features like multi-factor authentication, device identity verification, and secure onboarding. Robust IAM systems contribute to compliance with data protection regulations and enhance the trustworthiness of cloud-connected IoT networks.

79. What are serverless architectures in the context of IoT cloud computing?

Answer: Serverless architectures allow developers to build and deploy applications without managing server infrastructure. In IoT, this approach enables lightweight, event-driven solutions where code runs in response to events such as data arrival from sensors. Services like AWS Lambda, Azure Functions, and Google Cloud Functions support serverless models, allowing developers to focus on functionality rather than infrastructure. Serverless computing scales automatically, charges based on actual usage, and reduces operational complexity. It is ideal for applications with fluctuating workloads, such as real-time data processing or scheduled device updates. This leads to faster development cycles and cost-effective deployment in IoT ecosystems.

80. How does blockchain enhance security in IoT and cloud environments?
Answer: Blockchain enhances security in IoT and cloud environments by providing a decentralized, immutable ledger for recording transactions and data exchanges. In IoT, blockchain can verify the identity and integrity of devices, prevent data tampering, and ensure secure peer-to-peer communication. It eliminates the need for centralized trust authorities, reducing single points of failure. Smart contracts can automate processes like device authentication, access control, and payment for data usage. In cloud computing, blockchain supports transparent auditing and data provenance. By combining cryptographic techniques with decentralized consensus mechanisms, blockchain offers robust security, trust, and traceability in connected digital ecosystems.

81. What is edge analytics in IoT?
Answer: Edge analytics refers to the process of collecting, analyzing, and interpreting data directly at the edge of the IoT network, near the source of data generation. Instead of sending all data to centralized cloud servers, edge analytics allows devices like sensors or gateways to process information locally. This reduces latency, enhances real-time decision-making, and lowers bandwidth consumption. It's particularly useful in time-sensitive applications such as autonomous vehicles, industrial automation, and health monitoring systems. By performing analytics at the edge, businesses can respond more quickly to events while reducing the load on cloud infrastructure and improving system efficiency.

82. How is a data lake useful in IoT cloud platforms?
Answer: A data lake is a centralized repository that allows storage of structured, semi-structured, and unstructured data at any scale. In IoT cloud platforms, data lakes are used to store massive volumes of raw sensor data, logs, audio, images, or videos from connected devices. Unlike traditional databases, data lakes are highly scalable and flexible, enabling advanced analytics and machine learning on diverse datasets. They support real-time as well as historical analysis, making them ideal for IoT applications like predictive maintenance, user behavior tracking, and smart city management. Popular cloud data lake services include AWS Lake Formation and Azure Data Lake.

83. What are IoT device twins in cloud computing?
Answer: IoT device twins are digital replicas of physical devices maintained in the cloud. They store real-time data about the state, metadata, configuration, and telemetry of the corresponding physical devices. Services like Azure IoT Hub and AWS IoT Device Shadow provide device twin functionality. These twins allow remote monitoring, diagnostics, and control, even when the physical device is temporarily offline. They facilitate simulation, testing, and predictive maintenance. Device twins bridge the gap between the physical and digital worlds, improving system observability, enabling synchronization, and simplifying device management in large-scale IoT deployments.

84. What is fog computing and how does it differ from edge computing?
Answer: Fog computing is an architectural approach where data processing and storage occur between the edge devices and the centralized cloud, typically at network gateways or routers. While edge computing performs processing directly on devices or sensors, fog computing introduces an intermediate layer for additional processing. Fog nodes manage latency-sensitive tasks and reduce the data volume sent to the cloud. It offers enhanced security, scalability, and control in distributed environments. Fog computing is especially useful in applications like autonomous vehicles, smart grids, and industrial IoT, where both real-time response and broader network management are critical.

85. What is MQTT and why is it widely used in IoT?
Answer: MQTT (Message Queuing Telemetry Transport) is a lightweight messaging protocol designed for low-bandwidth, high-latency, or unreliable networks—common in IoT systems. Based on the publish-subscribe model, MQTT enables efficient and real-time communication between devices and servers. It minimizes overhead, making it ideal for battery-powered and constrained devices. The protocol ensures reliable message delivery through three

Quality of Service (QoS) levels and supports encrypted communication for security. Due to its simplicity and effectiveness, MQTT is widely used in smart homes, industrial automation, and health monitoring applications. Popular platforms like AWS IoT Core and IBM Watson IoT support MQTT natively.

86. What is the concept of elasticity in cloud computing?
Answer: Elasticity in cloud computing refers to the ability to dynamically allocate or release computing resources based on current demands. This ensures that applications have enough resources to perform optimally during peak loads and avoid unnecessary costs during idle times. Elasticity is crucial for IoT systems that experience fluctuating workloads, such as energy grids or weather monitoring platforms. It supports automatic scaling of storage, processing power, or networking resources, ensuring continuous performance without manual intervention. Elasticity enhances cost efficiency, availability, and responsiveness, making it a fundamental benefit of cloud computing over traditional infrastructures.

87. How does 5G technology benefit cloud-based IoT solutions?
Answer: 5G technology significantly enhances cloud-based IoT solutions by providing ultra-low latency, high-speed connectivity, and the capacity to connect billions of devices simultaneously. These features enable real-time data transmission and processing, which is vital for applications like autonomous vehicles, remote surgery, and industrial automation. 5G's improved bandwidth allows faster uploads to cloud platforms, ensuring seamless device-to-cloud integration. Its network slicing capability further enables the prioritization of critical IoT services. By combining 5G with cloud infrastructure, IoT systems become more scalable, efficient, and responsive, accelerating the adoption of smart city and Industry 4.0 applications.

88. What is the significance of SLA (Service Level Agreement) in cloud computing for IoT?
Answer: A Service Level Agreement (SLA) is a formal contract between a cloud service provider and a customer, outlining the expected level of service, including uptime, performance, support, and penalties for non-compliance. In IoT, where continuous device communication and data availability are crucial, SLAs ensure that cloud platforms meet the required reliability and performance standards. They also define metrics like response time, data durability, and security protocols. Having a clear SLA helps IoT businesses minimize downtime, maintain service quality, and hold providers accountable, thereby building trust and ensuring smooth operations.

89. What is the role of time-series databases in IoT cloud solutions?
Answer: Time-series databases (TSDBs) are optimized to store and retrieve time-stamped data, making them ideal for IoT applications where devices continuously generate data over time. They support high ingestion rates, efficient querying, and data compression. Examples include InfluxDB, TimescaleDB, and AWS Timestream. In IoT cloud solutions, TSDBs enable tracking of trends, anomalies, and performance metrics in systems like smart meters, environmental sensors, and industrial equipment. Their ability to handle large-scale, chronological data efficiently makes them essential for real-time analytics, forecasting, and alerting in IoT ecosystems.

90. What is device provisioning in IoT cloud platforms?
Answer: Device provisioning is the process of registering, configuring, and connecting IoT devices securely to a cloud platform. It involves assigning unique identities, setting credentials, defining policies, and establishing communication protocols. Automated provisioning streamlines onboarding of thousands of devices while maintaining security and compliance. Cloud services like AWS IoT Core and Azure IoT Hub offer tools for bulk provisioning and lifecycle management. Proper provisioning ensures that devices are authenticated, authorized, and ready to exchange data, reducing manual effort and minimizing deployment errors in large IoT networks.

91. What is the difference between vertical and horizontal scaling in cloud for IoT?
Answer: Vertical scaling (scaling up) refers to increasing the capacity of a single cloud instance, such as adding more CPU or RAM. Horizontal scaling (scaling out) involves adding more instances or nodes to distribute the workload. In IoT, vertical scaling may suit centralized applications with heavy processing needs, while horizontal scaling is ideal for systems handling numerous concurrent device connections. Cloud platforms offer autoscaling features for both approaches. Horizontal scaling provides better fault tolerance and flexibility, making it more suitable for distributed IoT environments that require high availability and rapid responsiveness.

92. What are the environmental impacts of IoT and how can cloud help mitigate them?

Answer: IoT devices can significantly impact the environment due to energy consumption, electronic waste, and data center emissions. However, cloud computing can help mitigate these effects by centralizing processing in energy-efficient data centers, supporting resource optimization, and enabling remote monitoring to reduce physical operations. Cloud analytics can also identify patterns to optimize energy usage in smart homes and factories. Moreover, IoT systems deployed for environmental monitoring, such as air quality sensors or waste management devices, benefit from cloud-enabled analytics to drive sustainability efforts and reduce carbon footprints.

93. What is the role of containerization in deploying IoT cloud applications?
Answer: Containerization packages applications and their dependencies into lightweight, portable containers, ensuring consistency across environments. In IoT cloud applications, containers enable rapid deployment, scalability, and resource efficiency. Tools like Docker and Kubernetes allow developers to run services reliably across edge, fog, and cloud infrastructure. Containers support microservices architectures, where each component (e.g., data processing, analytics, storage) operates independently, facilitating updates and fault isolation. This modularity is ideal for dynamic IoT ecosystems that require fast adaptation to changing workloads and technologies.

94. What is a digital twin and how is it used in cloud IoT platforms?
Answer: A digital twin is a virtual model of a physical asset, process, or system that mirrors its real-world counterpart using real-time IoT data. Cloud platforms use digital twins to simulate, analyze, and predict system behavior. In manufacturing, a digital twin of machinery helps monitor wear and predict maintenance needs. In smart cities, twins of infrastructure help optimize traffic or energy distribution. Digital twins enhance operational efficiency, reduce downtime, and support innovation through virtual testing and scenario analysis. They rely on robust IoT-cloud integration to remain synchronized and effective.

95. How does real-time data streaming work in cloud-based IoT?
Answer: Real-time data streaming in cloud-based IoT involves continuous transmission of data from devices to cloud services for immediate processing and analysis. Tools like Apache Kafka, AWS Kinesis, and Azure Event Hubs enable the ingestion of high-speed data streams. These platforms buffer, route, and process data in real time, allowing applications to respond instantly to changes. For example, streaming data from industrial sensors can trigger alerts when temperature thresholds are breached. Real-time streaming enhances responsiveness, enables automation, and improves situational awareness in mission-critical IoT systems.

96. What are over-the-air (OTA) updates in IoT cloud systems?
Answer: Over-the-air (OTA) updates refer to the remote distribution and installation of firmware, software, or configuration changes on IoT devices via cloud platforms. OTA updates allow vendors to fix bugs, patch security vulnerabilities, or add new features without requiring physical access. They are essential for maintaining device security, performance, and functionality over time. Cloud IoT services manage OTA campaigns, ensuring safe and scalable rollout to thousands of devices. Secure OTA mechanisms include digital signatures and encrypted transmission to prevent unauthorized updates and ensure integrity.

97. What is the significance of interoperability in IoT cloud ecosystems?
Answer: Interoperability ensures that different IoT devices, platforms, and applications can communicate and work together seamlessly. In cloud ecosystems, this allows integration of diverse hardware, protocols, and vendors into a unified system. It fosters innovation, reduces vendor lock-in, and accelerates deployment. Standards like MQTT, CoAP, and OPC UA, along with open APIs, facilitate interoperability. Cloud platforms further enhance this by providing SDKs, connectors, and cross-platform support. Ensuring interoperability is critical for creating scalable, flexible, and future-proof IoT solutions.

98. What is a smart contract and how is it applied in IoT-cloud integration?
Answer: A smart contract is a self-executing program stored on a blockchain that automatically enforces the terms of an agreement when predefined conditions are met. In IoT-cloud integration, smart contracts enable autonomous and secure interactions between devices without human intervention. For example, in supply chains, a smart contract can trigger payment once a shipment is verified by IoT sensors. This enhances trust, reduces delays, and prevents fraud. Combining IoT with blockchain and smart contracts opens new possibilities for automation and decentralized operations across industries.

99. What are microservices and why are they important in IoT cloud platforms?

Answer: Microservices are a software architecture style where an application is broken into small, independent services that communicate via APIs. In IoT cloud platforms, microservices offer flexibility, scalability, and maintainability. Each microservice can handle a specific function such as data ingestion, device management, or analytics. This allows teams to develop, deploy, and scale components independently, accelerating innovation and reducing downtime. Microservices also improve fault tolerance—if one service fails, others continue to operate. Their modular design makes them ideal for complex, evolving IoT systems.

100. What is IoT device lifecycle management in the cloud?
Answer: IoT device lifecycle management involves overseeing all stages of a device's life—from provisioning and configuration to maintenance and decommissioning—via cloud platforms. It includes device registration, monitoring, firmware updates, diagnostics, and retirement. Lifecycle management ensures security, compliance, and optimal performance throughout the device's operational span. Cloud platforms provide centralized tools for bulk onboarding, health tracking, and automated updates. Effective lifecycle management minimizes operational overhead, extends device longevity, and supports scalability and resilience in large-scale IoT deployments.

101. What is service orchestration in cloud computing?
Answer: Service orchestration in cloud computing refers to the coordinated management and automation of various services and processes across a cloud environment. It involves integrating different components such as storage, compute, networking, and applications into a single workflow that meets specific business requirements. Orchestration ensures that services interact correctly, resources are allocated efficiently, and dependencies are maintained. Tools like Kubernetes, Apache Airflow, and AWS CloudFormation are commonly used. Effective orchestration simplifies complex operations, improves scalability, and enhances system reliability by automating repetitive tasks and dynamically managing workloads in a distributed environment.

102. What are virtual private clouds (VPCs)?
Answer: A Virtual Private Cloud (VPC) is a secure, isolated section of a public cloud where users can deploy resources such as virtual machines, storage, and databases. VPCs provide users with control over network configurations, including IP address ranges, subnets, route tables, and gateways. This enables businesses to mimic a traditional on-premise network while benefiting from the scalability and flexibility of the cloud. VPCs support private and public subnets, firewalls, and security groups to regulate traffic. Major cloud providers like AWS, Google Cloud, and Azure offer VPC capabilities, enhancing security, compliance, and data control.

103. How is disaster recovery managed in cloud environments?
Answer: Disaster recovery in cloud environments is managed through strategies that ensure business continuity during unexpected failures or disasters. This includes regular data backups, redundant systems, geographic replication, and automated failover mechanisms. Cloud providers offer Disaster Recovery as a Service (DRaaS), enabling rapid recovery of infrastructure and applications. Recovery Time Objective (RTO) and Recovery Point Objective (RPO) are critical metrics in planning. Cloud-based recovery is cost-effective, scalable, and faster compared to traditional methods. It allows businesses to restore operations with minimal downtime and data loss, ensuring resilience and customer trust.

104. What is fog computing in the context of IoT?
Answer: Fog computing is a decentralized computing infrastructure that extends cloud computing capabilities closer to IoT devices and edge nodes. It processes data locally or near the data source instead of relying solely on centralized cloud servers. This reduces latency, improves response times, and decreases bandwidth usage. Fog computing is ideal for time-sensitive applications like autonomous vehicles, smart grids, and healthcare monitoring. It provides enhanced security, real-time analytics, and local decision-making capabilities. By bridging the gap between IoT devices and the cloud, fog computing supports more efficient and scalable IoT implementations.

105. What are containers in cloud computing?
Answer: Containers in cloud computing are lightweight, portable units that package an application and its dependencies into a single executable image. Unlike virtual machines, containers share the host operating system kernel, making them more resource-efficient. Tools like Docker and Kubernetes enable container creation, deployment, and management. Containers support microservices architecture and DevOps practices, facilitating faster development, testing, and scaling of applications. They ensure consistent environments across development and

production, reduce overhead, and improve scalability. Containers are widely used in cloud-native applications for their portability, isolation, and quick startup times.

106. How does big data analytics integrate with cloud computing?
Answer: Big data analytics integrates seamlessly with cloud computing by utilizing cloud infrastructure to store, process, and analyze large volumes of structured and unstructured data. Cloud platforms offer scalable storage and high-performance computing, which are essential for handling big data workloads. Services like Amazon EMR, Google BigQuery, and Azure HDInsight allow businesses to run analytics on petabyte-scale datasets without heavy upfront investments. Cloud-based big data tools enable real-time insights, predictive analytics, and machine learning. This integration supports data-driven decision-making, reduces costs, and enhances business agility in dynamic environments.

107. What is network slicing in IoT and cloud ecosystems?
Answer: Network slicing is a technique that enables the creation of multiple virtual networks over a single physical infrastructure, each tailored for specific applications or services. In IoT and cloud ecosystems, it allows for differentiated quality of service (QoS) based on latency, bandwidth, and security needs. For instance, a slice for autonomous vehicles requires low latency, while another for video streaming needs high bandwidth. Network slicing enhances resource utilization, supports diverse IoT use cases, and facilitates 5G deployment. It ensures efficient network management, better user experience, and scalability for varied service requirements.

108. What is API management in cloud services?
Answer: API management in cloud services refers to the process of designing, publishing, monitoring, and securing APIs that facilitate communication between different cloud services and applications. It includes tools for authentication, rate limiting, traffic monitoring, and analytics. API gateways serve as intermediaries that manage requests and enforce policies. Effective API management ensures seamless integration, improves developer experience, and enhances security. It supports service monetization, scalability, and lifecycle management. Cloud providers like Azure API Management and AWS API Gateway offer robust tools to streamline API operations and enable digital transformation.

109. How does serverless architecture benefit cloud applications?
Answer: Serverless architecture enables developers to build and run applications without managing the underlying server infrastructure. In this model, cloud providers dynamically allocate resources and execute code in response to events or triggers. Benefits include automatic scaling, reduced operational complexity, and cost-efficiency, as users pay only for actual usage. Serverless platforms like AWS Lambda, Azure Functions, and Google Cloud Functions allow rapid development and deployment of microservices. This architecture is ideal for event-driven applications, such as real-time data processing or backend services, enhancing agility and time-to-market.

110. What are cloud-native applications?
Answer: Cloud-native applications are designed specifically to operate in cloud environments by leveraging cloud computing principles such as scalability, resilience, and elasticity. These applications use microservices architecture, containers, APIs, and continuous integration/continuous deployment (CI/CD) practices. Unlike traditional monolithic applications, cloud-native apps can be easily deployed, updated, and scaled independently. They are resilient to failures, optimized for dynamic infrastructure, and support rapid innovation. Cloud-native development enables organizations to respond quickly to market changes, reduce downtime, and deliver enhanced user experiences through agile and modular software development.

111. What is the role of artificial intelligence (AI) in cloud computing?
Answer: Artificial Intelligence (AI) enhances cloud computing by automating processes, optimizing resource allocation, and enabling advanced analytics. Cloud providers offer AI services like machine learning models, natural language processing, and computer vision tools through platforms like AWS SageMaker, Azure AI, and Google AI. These services allow developers to integrate intelligent features into applications without extensive expertise. AI improves cloud operations through predictive maintenance, anomaly detection, and auto-scaling. It also supports smarter decision-making, personalized user experiences, and faster data processing, making cloud platforms more adaptive, efficient, and intelligent.

112. How does blockchain integrate with IoT and cloud systems?

Answer: Blockchain integrates with IoT and cloud systems by providing decentralized, tamper-proof ledgers that enhance data security, transparency, and trust. In IoT, blockchain ensures the integrity of data exchanged between devices, prevents unauthorized access, and supports audit trails. Combined with cloud computing, blockchain enables secure sharing of data across distributed networks. Applications include smart contracts, supply chain tracking, and secure device authentication. This integration addresses challenges like data breaches and privacy concerns, promoting reliable communication and automation in multi-device environments without relying solely on central authorities.

113. What is the difference between vertical and horizontal scaling in cloud computing?
Answer: Vertical scaling, or scaling up, involves increasing the capacity of a single server or instance by adding more CPU, RAM, or storage. It is simple but limited by the hardware's maximum capacity. Horizontal scaling, or scaling out, involves adding more servers or instances to distribute the workload. It provides greater flexibility and fault tolerance. Cloud platforms support both methods, though horizontal scaling is more suited for high-availability and distributed systems. Choosing the right scaling strategy depends on application architecture, cost considerations, and performance requirements in a dynamic environment.

114. What is a multi-cloud strategy?
Answer: A multi-cloud strategy involves using services from multiple cloud providers simultaneously, such as AWS, Azure, and Google Cloud, to avoid vendor lock-in, enhance redundancy, and leverage the best offerings from each provider. This approach improves resilience, reduces dependency on a single provider, and supports compliance with regional regulations. However, it also introduces challenges in data integration, security, and management complexity. Organizations adopt multi-cloud strategies to optimize performance, cost, and innovation. Successful implementation requires robust cloud governance, monitoring tools, and skilled personnel to manage heterogeneous environments.

115. How do IoT platforms manage device provisioning and updates?
Answer: IoT platforms manage device provisioning and updates by providing automated tools for onboarding new devices, assigning unique identities, and configuring initial settings. These platforms also support secure over-the-air (OTA) firmware updates, ensuring devices remain functional and protected against vulnerabilities. Device management includes monitoring, diagnostics, remote control, and lifecycle tracking. Leading IoT platforms like AWS IoT Core and Azure IoT Hub offer scalable solutions for managing millions of connected devices. Effective provisioning and update mechanisms are crucial for maintaining system reliability, security, and scalability in IoT deployments.

116. What is cloud interoperability and why is it important?
Answer: Cloud interoperability refers to the ability of different cloud services and platforms to work together seamlessly, allowing data exchange, workload migration, and application integration across providers. It is essential for preventing vendor lock-in, enhancing flexibility, and promoting collaboration. Interoperability supports hybrid and multi-cloud strategies, enabling organizations to combine services based on performance and cost benefits. Standards like REST APIs, containers, and open-source frameworks foster interoperability. Ensuring cloud systems are interoperable improves efficiency, reduces operational silos, and supports future-proof, agile IT infrastructure.

117. What are the challenges of IoT security?
Answer: IoT security faces challenges due to the vast number of connected devices, limited computing resources, and heterogeneous architectures. Common issues include weak authentication, unsecured communication protocols, firmware vulnerabilities, and lack of regular updates. Cyberattacks like DDoS, data breaches, and device hijacking are prevalent. Ensuring IoT security requires strong encryption, access control, secure boot mechanisms, and continuous monitoring. Regulatory compliance, device lifecycle management, and user awareness also play critical roles. Addressing these challenges is vital to protect sensitive data, ensure system integrity, and build user trust in IoT solutions.

118. What is edge AI in IoT?
Answer: Edge AI refers to deploying artificial intelligence models directly on IoT edge devices, enabling data processing and decision-making close to the data source. This approach reduces latency, conserves bandwidth, and enhances privacy by minimizing data transmission to centralized cloud servers. Edge AI supports real-time applications like video analytics, predictive maintenance, and autonomous vehicles. It requires optimized models, efficient hardware, and reliable inference engines. Technologies like TensorFlow Lite and NVIDIA Jetson facilitate

edge AI deployment. Combining AI with edge computing transforms IoT into a more intelligent, responsive, and decentralized ecosystem.

119. How is container orchestration used in cloud computing?

Answer: Container orchestration is the automated management of containerized applications across multiple hosts. It involves scheduling, scaling, networking, and health monitoring of containers to ensure high availability and reliability. Kubernetes is the most popular container orchestration platform, enabling developers to manage clusters efficiently. Orchestration simplifies deployment, rolling updates, and resource allocation, making it essential for microservices-based architectures. It enhances fault tolerance, load balancing, and service discovery in dynamic environments. With container orchestration, organizations can maintain consistent performance, reduce downtime, and streamline DevOps workflows in cloud-native applications.

120. What is cloud bursting and how does it work?

Answer: Cloud bursting is a hybrid cloud configuration where an application primarily runs in a private cloud or data center but temporarily bursts into a public cloud during peak demand. This model allows businesses to handle unexpected traffic surges without overprovisioning private infrastructure. It is cost-effective and enhances scalability. When internal resources are maxed out, additional workloads are redirected to public cloud instances. Cloud bursting requires compatibility between environments, secure data transfer, and seamless orchestration. It is ideal for non-sensitive, variable workloads and supports business continuity during traffic spikes.

121. What is the role of DevOps in cloud computing?

Answer: DevOps plays a critical role in cloud computing by facilitating continuous integration and continuous delivery (CI/CD) of software applications. It brings development and operations teams together to streamline the software development lifecycle, automate deployments, and monitor application performance. In the cloud, DevOps enables agile practices like version control, infrastructure as code (IaC), automated testing, and rollback mechanisms. Tools such as Jenkins, GitHub Actions, Terraform, and Ansible are widely used. Cloud-native DevOps enhances scalability, accelerates release cycles, reduces errors, and improves collaboration, resulting in faster innovation and efficient resource utilization.

122. What is the concept of Identity and Access Management (IAM) in cloud?

Answer: Identity and Access Management (IAM) in cloud computing is a framework of policies and technologies that ensures only authorized individuals and systems have access to cloud resources. IAM helps manage user identities, roles, and permissions, ensuring secure authentication and authorization across services. Cloud providers like AWS, Azure, and GCP offer IAM tools that include multi-factor authentication, least-privilege access, role-based access control (RBAC), and policy enforcement. Effective IAM mitigates security risks, prevents unauthorized access, and ensures compliance with organizational and regulatory standards.

123. What are cloud-native databases and how are they different?

Answer: Cloud-native databases are databases designed specifically to run in cloud environments, leveraging cloud-native principles such as scalability, elasticity, high availability, and multi-tenancy. Unlike traditional databases that require manual provisioning and scaling, cloud-native databases are managed services that auto-scale, handle failovers, and provide built-in backups. Examples include Amazon Aurora, Google Cloud Spanner, and Azure Cosmos DB. These databases support distributed architectures, containerization, and microservices integration. They offer flexibility, global accessibility, and lower maintenance overhead, making them ideal for dynamic cloud applications and modern software development.

124. How do real-time analytics work in IoT applications?

Answer: Real-time analytics in IoT applications involve collecting, processing, and analyzing data from IoT devices instantly as it is generated. This enables immediate decision-making, anomaly detection, and triggering of automated actions. Edge computing and stream processing tools like Apache Kafka, AWS Kinesis, and Azure Stream Analytics are used to process data near the source. Real-time analytics is essential in use cases like smart manufacturing, traffic management, and healthcare monitoring. It helps organizations improve operational efficiency, reduce response time, and enhance safety by reacting to events as they occur.

125. What is the significance of MQTT protocol in IoT?

Answer: MQTT (Message Queuing Telemetry Transport) is a lightweight messaging protocol designed for low-bandwidth, high-latency, or unreliable networks, making it ideal for IoT. It follows the publish-subscribe model, where devices (clients) publish messages to topics, and other devices subscribe to those topics. MQTT's small packet size, minimal overhead, and quality of service (QoS) levels allow efficient communication between IoT devices and servers. It is widely supported across platforms and preferred for remote monitoring, sensor data transmission, and mobile IoT applications due to its reliability and low resource consumption.

126. What are the different types of IoT networks?
Answer: IoT networks are classified based on range, bandwidth, and use case. Common types include:
PAN (Personal Area Network) – For short-range communication (e.g., Bluetooth).
LAN (Local Area Network) – For home automation or enterprise IoT systems.
WAN (Wide Area Network) – For long-range connectivity using cellular networks.
LPWAN (Low-Power Wide-Area Network) – Includes LoRaWAN, NB-IoT, and Sigfox, designed for low-power, long-range applications.
Mesh Networks – Devices relay data between one another, increasing reliability and range. Each network type supports different IoT needs, from wearables to industrial monitoring.

127. How does load balancing improve cloud application performance?
Answer: Load balancing distributes incoming network traffic across multiple servers or resources to ensure no single server becomes overwhelmed. In cloud computing, load balancers improve application performance, availability, and fault tolerance by automatically routing traffic based on server health and capacity. They support both Layer 4 (TCP) and Layer 7 (HTTP/HTTPS) traffic. Cloud providers offer load balancing services like AWS Elastic Load Balancer, Azure Load Balancer, and Google Cloud Load Balancing. These tools ensure optimal resource use, minimize downtime, and provide seamless user experiences during traffic spikes or failures.

128. What are digital twins in IoT?
Answer: A digital twin is a virtual representation of a physical object or system, created using real-time data from IoT sensors. It mimics the behavior and condition of its physical counterpart, allowing monitoring, diagnostics, and simulations. In industries like manufacturing, healthcare, and smart cities, digital twins are used for predictive maintenance, performance optimization, and testing scenarios without risking real assets. Integration with AI and analytics enhances insights and decision-making. Digital twins improve operational efficiency, reduce costs, and increase system reliability by enabling proactive responses to potential issues.

129. What is the role of artificial intelligence in IoT?
Answer: Artificial Intelligence (AI) enhances IoT by enabling devices and systems to process data intelligently, identify patterns, and make decisions without human intervention. AI techniques like machine learning, neural networks, and natural language processing are used in applications such as predictive maintenance, anomaly detection, image recognition, and speech processing. By analyzing real-time and historical IoT data, AI improves automation, user personalization, and efficiency. Combined with edge computing, AI enables low-latency, decentralized decision-making, making IoT systems smarter, more adaptive, and capable of handling complex tasks.

130. What is hybrid cloud and how is it beneficial?
Answer: A hybrid cloud is a computing environment that combines private cloud, public cloud, and on-premises infrastructure, allowing data and applications to move between them seamlessly. It provides flexibility, scalability, and cost-efficiency while maintaining control over sensitive data. Organizations use hybrid cloud to meet regulatory compliance, optimize workload placement, and ensure business continuity. Benefits include improved disaster recovery, better resource utilization, and reduced vendor lock-in. Tools like VMware Cloud, Azure Arc, and Google Anthos help manage hybrid environments effectively, offering unified visibility and policy enforcement across cloud and local resources.

131. What is a microcontroller and how is it used in IoT?
Answer: A microcontroller is a compact integrated circuit that contains a processor, memory, and input/output peripherals. It is the brain of many IoT devices, used for sensing, controlling, and communicating tasks. Microcontrollers collect data from sensors, process it, and trigger actions or communicate with other devices or the cloud. Examples include Arduino, ESP8266, and STM32. They are energy-efficient and cost-effective, making them

ideal for embedded IoT systems like smart thermostats, wearable devices, and environmental sensors. Their programmability allows customization for specific IoT applications.

132. What is geofencing in IoT?
Answer: Geofencing is a location-based service in IoT that creates a virtual boundary around a geographic area. When a device enters or exits this boundary, predefined actions are triggered, such as sending alerts or activating devices. Geofencing uses GPS, RFID, Wi-Fi, or cellular data to determine the device's location. It is widely used in fleet management, smart home automation, and security systems. For instance, a geofenced smart lock can automatically unlock when a user approaches home. This technology enhances convenience, security, and automation in IoT ecosystems.

133. What is Infrastructure as Code (IaC) in cloud computing?
Answer: Infrastructure as Code (IaC) is a DevOps practice that involves managing and provisioning cloud infrastructure using machine-readable configuration files instead of manual processes. IaC allows teams to define infrastructure components—such as servers, networks, and databases—as code, enabling version control, reproducibility, and automation. Tools like Terraform, AWS CloudFormation, and Ansible are used to implement IaC. It reduces configuration errors, speeds up deployments, and supports continuous delivery. By treating infrastructure like application code, organizations achieve greater agility, consistency, and scalability in managing cloud environments.

134. What are smart sensors in IoT and their role?
Answer: Smart sensors in IoT are advanced sensors equipped with embedded processors and communication interfaces. They not only sense physical parameters like temperature, humidity, or motion but also process data locally and transmit it to other devices or cloud platforms. Smart sensors support real-time monitoring, data filtering, and edge analytics. They are crucial in applications such as smart agriculture, healthcare monitoring, industrial automation, and environmental tracking. Their ability to make autonomous decisions and reduce data transmission helps conserve energy and bandwidth, making IoT systems more efficient and intelligent.

135. What is latency and why is it important in cloud and IoT?
Answer: Latency refers to the time delay between a user action or data request and the system's response. In cloud and IoT systems, low latency is crucial for applications that require real-time responses, such as autonomous vehicles, remote surgeries, or industrial control systems. High latency can lead to performance degradation, safety issues, or user dissatisfaction. Techniques like edge computing, content delivery networks (CDNs), and optimized network routing are used to reduce latency. Monitoring and minimizing latency ensures faster data processing, improved user experience, and operational efficiency.

136. How does Kubernetes enhance cloud computing?
Answer: Kubernetes is an open-source container orchestration platform that automates the deployment, scaling, and management of containerized applications. In cloud computing, it enables developers to manage complex applications across clusters of machines with ease. Kubernetes handles tasks like service discovery, load balancing, self-healing, and rolling updates. It abstracts infrastructure complexities and supports hybrid and multi-cloud environments. By improving resource utilization, enabling microservices architecture, and supporting continuous deployment, Kubernetes plays a vital role in building scalable, resilient, and efficient cloud-native applications.

137. What are cloud access security brokers (CASBs)?
Answer: Cloud Access Security Brokers (CASBs) are security enforcement points placed between cloud service consumers and providers to monitor and control access to cloud resources. CASBs provide visibility into cloud usage, enforce security policies, detect threats, and ensure compliance with regulations. They offer capabilities like data loss prevention (DLP), encryption, identity management, and anomaly detection. CASBs help organizations secure SaaS, IaaS, and PaaS applications across multiple platforms. They are essential in preventing data breaches, managing shadow IT, and maintaining governance in cloud environments.

138. What is the difference between synchronous and asynchronous communication in IoT?
Answer: In IoT, synchronous communication requires devices to send and receive data at the same time, ensuring real-time interaction. It is used in time-critical applications like remote surgeries or live monitoring. Asynchronous communication, on the other hand, allows devices to send data without waiting for an immediate response. It is suitable

for non-urgent tasks like data logging or delayed processing. Asynchronous methods are more bandwidth-efficient and scalable, while synchronous methods offer better responsiveness. The choice depends on the application's latency sensitivity and network conditions.

139. What are firmware-over-the-air (FOTA) updates in IoT?
Answer: Firmware-Over-The-Air (FOTA) updates enable remote updating of firmware on IoT devices via wireless communication. This approach eliminates the need for physical access, reduces maintenance costs, and ensures devices remain secure and functional. FOTA systems involve secure transmission, version control, and rollback mechanisms to prevent failures. They are vital for patching vulnerabilities, adding new features, and improving performance. Cloud-based FOTA solutions offer scheduling, monitoring, and analytics capabilities, enhancing scalability and operational efficiency in managing large IoT device fleets.

140. What is the significance of IPv6 in IoT?
Answer: IPv6 (Internet Protocol version 6) is crucial for IoT due to its vast address space, allowing trillions of devices to connect to the internet. Unlike IPv4, which is limited to approximately 4.3 billion addresses, IPv6 supports 340 undecillion addresses, making it ideal for the explosive growth of IoT. It also offers features like simplified packet headers, improved routing, and built-in security. IPv6 facilitates end-to-end device connectivity, scalability, and network efficiency. As IoT expands, adopting IPv6 becomes essential to accommodate future demands and ensure seamless global communication.

9 789369 725816

Printed at Repro India Ltd.